ROMAINE WASN'T BUILT IN A DAY

ROMAINE WASN'T BUILT IN A DAY

The Delightful History of FOOD LANGUAGE

JUDITH TSCHANN

Illustrations by Peter Tschann-Grimm

VORACIOUS

Little, Brown and Company
New York Boston London

Voracious / Little, Brown and Company
Hachette Book Group
1290 Avenue of the Americas, New York, NY 10104
littlebrown.com

First Edition: February 2023

Voracious is an imprint of Little, Brown and Company, a division of Hachette Book Group, Inc. The Voracious name and logo are trademarks of Hachette Book Group, Inc.

The publisher is not responsible for websites (or their content) that are not owned by the publisher.

The Hachette Speakers Bureau provides a wide range of authors for speaking events. To find out more, go to hachettespeakersbureau.com or email hachettespeakers@hbgusa.com.

Little, Brown and Company books may be purchased in bulk for business, educational, or promotional use. For information, please contact your local bookseller or the Hachette Book Group Special Markets Department at special.markets@hbgusa.com.

ISBN 9780316389372
LCCN 2022940004

Printing 1, 2022

LSC-C

Printed in the United States of America

For Mom

Contents

Ways of Reading This Book

Open the book at random, read a snippet or two, nod sagely, and go back to work.

Flip back and forth, find a few juicy bits—*avocado! Vanilla! Pumpernickel!* (pp. 55, 65, 94)—memorize the info, and amaze your friends at parties.

Pace around the room, book in one hand, gesturing wildly with the other, as you shriek with intellectual triumph: "So that's where the word *buccaneer* comes from! And I knew there was something odd about *partridge*" (pp. 164, 167).

Or read the old-fashioned way, straight through from beginning to end, "Breakfast" to "Nightcaps," at which point, though full, you will think fondly of tomorrow's meals and be grateful for the endless return of appetite.

ROMAINE WASN'T BUILT IN A DAY

Introduction

Eating and talking are two of our biggest pleasures. We talk all day, and some of us even talk in our sleep. We talk more than we eat, though we probably think about food more often than language. When we talk—whether using spoken words, or Protactile (a language of touch used by the DeafBlind community), or by signing, thumbing a message, or in some other way—we seldom think about the history of words or the ways that English has changed over the centuries or why English has such a wealth of synonyms.

But word lovers enjoy learning facts about language, just as foodies like to learn about eatables, comestibles, grub, chow, and vittles (to indulge in some of the many synonyms for food). One amusing way to learn about food is through the words we use for our daily meals. What a joy when the two loves overlap! It's a two-for-one deal, because learning the history of the food words—their etymologies—means learning at least some aspects of the foods' histories, like where they originated. (Note that ***boldface italics*** indicate the first occurrence of a food term whose origin is

A croissant moon

discussed in the book. Consult the index for page numbers of any subsequent occurrences with additional information.)

From that early-morning cuppa joe and croissant to a lunchtime taco, a dinner barbecue, and a late-night toddy and piece of pie, the details about a food's or a word's history often come with surprises.

Joe most likely comes from U.S. military slang for a soldier. The word *croissant* has a long history with many meanings, including the "waxing or waning moon" and, going back to the Latin word *crēscere*, "to grow."

Taco comes from Mexican Spanish and means "plug" or "wad"; it referred to part of an explosive used in silver mining. *Barbecue* comes from the Caribbean Arawakan word *barbacoa*, meaning "wooden frame for sleeping on and for drying food."

Toddy comes from the Hindi *tari,* "palm wine," and ***pie*** probably comes from a French word meaning "magpie," a bird that loves to collect objects. How did the junk heap of a magpie become the name of a delicious dessert?

Getting the scoop on *pie* or tracking down the history of any word can lead to eye-openers, if not always answers. Etymology can be both entertaining and enlightening, because a word's history is loaded with information—often about culture.

Take *sycophant,* for example. It meant "fig-showing" in Greek. We might say that a sycophant kisses up to someone (or we might use more colorful language), but in ancient Greece, a sycophant apparently "showed the fig" (a bit like giving the finger) to someone suspected of being an informer. Ancient nonverbal insults were not so different from our own.

Or consider the mundane word ***romaine.*** It comes from medieval French *laitue romaine,* "Roman lettuce." But a word or food sleuth doesn't want to stop with this answer, because one wonders, *What's Roman about this lettuce?*

The leafy green has been grown in the Mediterranean area since ancient times and in Rome since at least classical times. The French presumably learned about it or bought it from the Romans. We could leave it at that—English speakers borrowed the word *romaine* from the French.

But when, why, how? There's always a clue to scratch and sniff…

For example, a French book written around 1394 concerning wifely virtues and household management (see *The Good Wife's Guide* in Sources) provides information on cooking harbor porpoise and hedgehog as well as lettuce. Modern editors of the book suggest that *laitue d'Avignon,* "lettuce of Avignon," could be what we know today as romaine and that it was brought to France by popes from Rome.

What were the popes doing in Avignon? From the year 1309 to 1376, seven popes lived there rather than in Rome because of political hostilities. The nearly seventy years of this Avignon papacy were followed by some forty years of the Western Schism, a period during which there was a pope in Rome and an antipope in Avignon.

One product of this contentious period was a delicious wine. **Châteauneuf-du-Pape** ("the pope's new castle") originated in the papal vineyards of Avignon in the fourteenth century. The pope's castle would have had kitchen gardens, and it's reasonable to suppose that the lettuce grown there was the same lettuce that was grown in Rome. Perhaps the Avignon papacy helped spread greens as well as good wine. Why not conclude that the French term *laitue romaine* comes from this period of popes leaving Rome and

taking up residence in Avignon, and that the term then
evolved over time to the
shortened *romaine* that we
use today?

We can't, because the clues
don't rise to the level of evidence. And there are no dots
connecting the Avignon popes
to the term *romaine lettuce* that
shows up for the first time in English in 1577 or with the later short-
ened form. Searching for *romaine* is a reminder that false or
not-yet-proven etymologies can take on lives of their own, often
because they're appealing and make a good story.

Nevertheless, when we dive into the history of *romaine*, we
discover that even if clues don't yield an answer about the word's
origin, the hunt can be satisfying—for example, leading us to
delve deeper into the *schism* (from Greek *skhizein*, "to split") in
the Catholic Church brought on by rival popes and antipopes.
Or pointing us to a fascinating medieval book written, supposedly, by an old Parisian husband for his young bride, a book
that is chock-full of advice for her, like when and precisely how
to plant lettuce seeds. This fifteen-year-old wife had a huge work-

load. Maybe she didn't mind that her husband never finished the book.

The pleasures of pursuing this word's history also include the discovery that four thousand years ago in Egypt, romaine was a phallic symbol. Because it grows straight and tall and oozes a semen-like liquid, it was associated with the god of fertility, Min, and it was also considered an aphrodisiac.

Still more about mundane romaine: It is a modern rescue food for *manatees* (from Carib *manáti*), whose seagrasses are disappearing because of pollution.

Here's a smorgasbord of information to provide historical context for the etymologies in this book. Lick your chops and dig in.

A Quick History of the English Lexicon

The English *lexicon* ("vocabulary," from the Greek *lexis,* "word") is huge, partially because English speakers have borrowed from so many different languages. *Borrowed words* and *loanwords* are traditional terms for words that are introduced into one language from a different one. (The terms *borrow* and *loan* are not quite logical here, since a word can't simply be returned, like a library book.)

English has borrowed from an array of languages, including Latin, Greek, Sanskrit, Arabic, Turkish, Igbo, Bantu, Urdu, Mandarin, Khmer, Algonquian, Nahuatl, and many more, perhaps some three hundred and fifty. (Check the appendix, which lists more than four dozen languages from which English has borrowed food words.) English has been enriched by contact with languages from all around the globe, and food words alone show this.

The story of English traditionally begins with the migration of the Angles, Saxons, and Jutes from the Continent to Britain shortly before 500 CE (CE meaning "of the Common Era"; the era is sometimes designated AD, for *anno Domini,* "in the year of the Lord"). These newcomers spoke versions of a West Germanic language that became what we now call Old English (go, *Beowulf*!). The Angles, Saxons, and Jutes conquered and assimilated the Celtic people already inhabiting Britain, with the partial and qualified exception of those in Cornwall, Wales, and Scotland.

In this Old English period (approximately 500 to 1100), barely two dozen Celtic words (*crag* is one of them) were absorbed into English, along with Celtic-based place-names like *London, Thames,* and *Avon.* A number of Latin words were also absorbed into English, especially words pertaining to religion, such as *bishop* and *martyr* (both ultimately Greek words but borrowed via Latin). Food words, including *fig* (Old English *fic,* meaning "hemorrhoid" as well as "fig"), **lobster, oyster,** and **ginger,** were also borrowed from Latin in this period (though *fig* was borrowed again later from Old French *fige.* For the source of *ginger,* see p. 183). With the arrival of the Vikings beginning in the eighth century, many Norse words entered English, including common words like *sky, skirt, fellow, both, same, take, get,* and *dirt,* and food words like **cake** and **egg.** The Old English word for *egg*—*ei*—remained in use along with the Norse word until early modern times, some people saying *ei,* some saying *egg,* and many lamenting the fact that everyone didn't use the same word. (For an *egg* versus *ei* story, see p. 68.)

During the Middle English period (1100 to 1450), thousands of French and Latin words became English, largely as a result of the Norman Conquest in 1066. *Normans* were "Northmen," Vikings who had settled in Normandy a few centuries earlier and given up Norse for a dialect of French. William the Conqueror and his barons spoke Norman French, and for centuries after the invaders took control of England, a language split was the norm, with kings, aristocrats, and social climbers speaking French and almost everyone else speaking English (again, there were some exceptions—Cornish was spoken in Cornwall, Welsh in Wales, and Scottish Gaelic in Scotland, although Scotland hadn't yet united with England).

During these centuries of French versus English, however, the nobility lost land and connections in France, and English nationalism grew; eventually, English was spoken by all classes, including the monarchy. In 1362, English was used at the opening of Parliament. During the Peasants' Revolt of 1381, Richard II addressed the rebels in English. (Rebel leader Wat Tyler talked back and was killed.) By 1400, the English language had won.

English not only prevailed but grew immensely, adding thousands of French words to its lexicon. Many of these pertained to law, courtly behavior, and religion, including *government, parliament, tax, crime, jury, verdict, fashion, gown, dance, leisure, palace, mansion, sermon, clergy, friar*. Others pertained to food: ***beef, cinnamon, cloves, dinner, fruit, gravy, lemon, nutmeg, mustard, orange,*** *pie,* ***poultry, pork, rice, sausage, spinach, sugar, veal, table, saucer, goblet, feast, supper,*** and many more. Some of these words (notably those for spices and citrus fruit), though they were adopted from French, derive ultimately from Arabic or Persian, entering English after a long and circuitous route through many languages, reflecting complex trade networks (for example, see *orange,* p. 61).

The Renaissance and early modern English period (1450 to 1800) brought another flood of words into English as a result of colonialism, exploration, and extensive trade: *arsenal, assassin, hashish, monsoon, sofa,* and the food words ***apricot, coffee,*** and ***sherbet*** came from Arabic; *barbecue,* ***chocolate, cocoa, hominy, pecan, pone, potato, quinoa, squash, tomato,*** came from indigenous languages of the Americas; ***poi*** came from Hawaiian;

banana and *yam* came from western African languages; *curry* came from Tamil; *ketchup* and *tea* came from Chinese, probably via Malay; *asparagus* came from Greek via Latin; *broccoli* and *macaroni* came from Italian; *whiskey* came from Scottish Gaelic or Irish Gaelic; *naan* came from Urdu; and *yogurt* came from Turkish.

During this early modern English period, a renewed interest in Western classical texts led to a fashion among some writers to invent fancy-sounding words formed from Greek and Latin roots. One such word, *fatigate* ("to tire someone"), didn't last. A great many others did, including *lexicon, education, system, chaos, chronology,* and *dogma.*

In modern English times (from 1800 to the present), science, medicine, technology, philosophy, the arts, pop culture, and other domains have contributed thousands of words to the English lexicon. A mere sampling of those words, most from the past hundred years: *taxonomy, electron, symbiosis, chlorophyll, robotics, cyberspace, bandwidth, bitcoin, cryptocurrency, internet, e-mail, sexting,* **byte** (see chapter 2 for food words in the digital world), *cubism, existentialism, jazz, bebop, pop, hip-hop, grunge, K-pop, meme, meta, selfie, baby boomer, glamping, poggers, amirite, GOAT.*

Here's a selection of food words borrowed in the nineteenth century: **bagel, bok choy, chow mein, gumbo, hot dog, hamburger, jerky, luau, pasta, pizza, sushi, spaghetti.** In the twentieth century, these food words entered the language: **bibimbap, boba, burrito, chimichanga, harissa, hummus, jollof, pho,** *taco,* **tzimmes, umami, wonton.**

Not all food terms in English were borrowed. Some, like **bread** and **beer,** are native — that is, Old English or pre-English Germanic words. And many words have entered the lexicon through compounding within English (for example, *bar* plus *tender* led to *bartender*); through back-formation (**pea,** from *pease,* which was a singular word that sounded plural, so eventually the *s* was dropped); slang (*slider* came from *small hamburger*); blending (*breakfast* plus *lunch* became *brunch*), and coining (*Sex on the Beach* and other cocktail names). Coining doesn't account for very many words, and it's different from other ways in which a vocabulary grows. It's done consciously, sometimes by committee, and it's often a matter of advertising and marketing.

Brand names are an example of coining, and occasionally these names lose their proprietary sense and become common words. For some people, *Kleenex* means any tissue. For millennials and others, the luxury brand Gucci has become an adjective — "It's all *Gucci,*" meaning "It's all good."

Google has gone from a proprietary name to a verb: "I *googled* it and found all sorts of dirt." (New verbs in English must form the past tense and past participle with *-ed*. Some verbs already in the language are irregular, like *sing, sang, sung,* but one can't say, for instance, "I gaggle it yesterday" or "I have often guggle his name.") The word *googol,* meaning the number one followed by a hundred zeros, was a kid's creation. Milton Sirotta, nine-year-old nephew of the mathematician Edward Kasner, coined it around 1920; Kasner and James Newman popularized the word in their 1940 *Mathematics and the Imagination.* In 1998, an internet company took the name Google, apparently by adopting and respelling *googol,* and since then, *google* has gone global.

The brand name **Jell-O** is often written *jello,* as in *jello shots* (alcohol-laced gelatin), and for many people it's a generic term for gelatin. Likewise, **granola** is a common word for cereal with mixed grains and fruits, but it was originally a proprietary name coined by W. K. Kellogg (see p. 65). And the little cake called **Twinkie** gave rise to the term *Twinkie defense,* which in 1979 meant "an excuse of criminal behavior because of excessive sugar consumption" and now means any "unconvincing, silly excuse."

The English lexicon has fattened from centuries of sucking up words from other languages. How many words does it have? A big desk dictionary might have 250,000 words, an online dictionary 500,000 with more added every day, and it's not unreasonable to suppose that English has more than a million words.

What counts as an English word? (Linguists talk about *lexemes* rather than *words;* google it if you're interested.) In this book, a word is part of the English lexicon if it appears in a big dictionary (see Sources), English-language newspapers, magazines, cookbooks, blogs, or other published writing, and if it usually appears without italics.

Dictionaries always lag behind spoken language, and linguists work hard compiling and analyzing immense databases of written and recorded speech, taking note of class, age, and other factors and trying to keep up with developments in all the varieties of English used around the world — in Great Britain, India, Hong Kong, Australia, New Zealand, Canada, the United States, South Africa, and elsewhere.

English is global, and so is the diet of many English speakers. And yet obviously people who speak English don't all talk the same way, use the same vocabulary, or share the same tastes. Ways of talking and diets are shaped by family tradition, friends, where people live, what resources they have, and many other particulars of their lives.

The various chapters in *Romaine Wasn't Built in a Day* explore some common and a few uncommon breakfast foods; computer terms taken from food; lunch words based on place-names, peo-ple's names, and body parts; happy-hour drinks with noteworthy names; dinner food both raw and cooked; and nightcaps that are sleep-inducing or aphrodisiacs. The final chapter broadens the focus from individual words to expressions using food metaphors, providing an opportunity to ruminate on how food language can define us.

With so many words in the English language, it is impossible to address every interesting etymology there is (and one could argue that *every* etymology is interesting). If your favorite food is not included in these pages, look it up while you cook it up and scribble the food word's origin in the margins.

Here are ten different ways people around the world say "Enjoy your meal." Match the expression to its language.

1. *Smakelijk eten*	(a) Yiddish
2. 食飯 *Sihk faahn*	(b) Navajo
3. *Meshiagare*	(c) Bosnian
4. *Prijatno*	(d) Cantonese
5. *Es gezunterheyt*	(e) Dutch
6. *Nizhonigo adiiyjit*	(f) Japanese
7. *'Anhcheunh pisaa oyy ban chhngeanh*	(g) Igbo

8. *Kainan na*   (h) Hindi

9. *Kripya bhojan ka anand lijiyai*   (i) Tagalog

10. *Rie nke oma*   (j) Khmer

Answers: 1 (e), 2 (d), 3 (f), 4 (c), 5 (a), 6 (b), 7 (j), 8 (i), 9 (h), 10 (g)

Two correct answers: genius

More than two: stupendous polyglot

1

Breakfast

Word Origins of Our Morning Fare

Some believe fasting is essential for good health and should be a nightly occurrence — no nibbling between dinner and breakfast. But whether you snack at night or not, the word used for the first meal of the day echoes the idea of having fasted.

Breakfast derives from Old English *brecan,* "to break" (going back to the Indo-European root *bhreg-,* "to break"; for more on Indo-European, see p. 41), and from Old Norse *fasta,* "a fast" or "period of abstaining from food." But even though the parts of this compound word go back to the early days of English, the word *breakfast* didn't come into use until the early modern period.

What did people call the first meal of the day if not *breakfast?*

In Old English times, people said *morgenmete,* "morning meal," and *morȝe-mete,* "morrow meal." (*Mete* meant "food" very broadly. The word narrowed over time to mean only "meat.") These and similar terms, like *morne-drynke,* continued to be used for centuries to refer to morning fare.

But the word *dinner,* which appeared in English in the thirteenth century, was also used to refer to breakfast. The *Middle English Dictionary* defines *dinner* as the first big meal of the day, usually eaten between nine a.m. and noon.

Dinner at nine o'clock in the morning?

Yes, as the history of the word suggests. *Dine* and *dinner* go back to the Latin *disjējūnāre* or *disiēiūnāre,* "to break one's fast." (Compare the modern English word *jejune,* meaning "naive, uninteresting," from Latin *jējūnus,* "empty, without food, not nourishing.") Many medieval people ate only two big meals a day, and midmorning dinner was one of them. Early risers (just about everyone) and workers in the field probably had a bite to eat before that. By the end of the Middle Ages, the term *breakfast* came to be used for the first meal, whether big or small, and the word *dinner* was used for a later meal, whether midday or evening.

What English speakers call *breakfast,* others around the world refer to as "morning meal," as in Japanese *asagohan* and Hebrew *aruchat boker.* A variation on that is the German *frühstück,* or "early bit." Turkish *kahvaltı* means "before or under coffee," suggesting food comes before the coffee. In Khmer (Cambodian), the first meal of the day is *ahar pelopruk,* "food in the morning," but that's a bit formal. It's more common to say *nham bai,* "eat rice." "Have you eaten rice yet?" is a common Khmer greeting at any time of day.

Of ten common words for breakfast fare — *coffee, tea, juice, cream, sugar, bread, bananas* or other *fruit, cereal,* and *ham* — only *bread* and *ham* go back to Old English. The other eight are borrowed from Arabic, French, Greek, Latin, Malay, and Mande (a branch of the Niger-Congo language family). The food people eat for breakfast shows how global English is — Old English words alongside words from languages around the world. Perhaps as much as 80 percent of our lexicon is borrowed.

Off the Menu: Breakfast and Voting

For some, *fat* is an F-word associated with breakfast — which makes sense if breakfast is bacon and doughnuts. In a different, etymological sense, the word *breakfast* is associated with many other F-words. *Fractal, fracture, fragile, fragment,* and *infringe* all share with *breakfast* the same Indo-European root: *bhreg-,* "to break." They're cognates, cousin words that came from the same ancestor. In the case of *bhreg-,* its descendants all involve the idea of breaking. The word *suffrage* is also a cousin of these F-words — ignore for a moment the *suf-* prefix, and the connection with the other words is clearer. What does the right to vote have to do with breaking? *Suffrage* comes from Latin *suffrāgārī,* "to vote for," from *frangere,* "to break" or *fragor,* "crash, breaking noise." *Suffrāgārī* may reflect ancient voting practices of casting pot shards as ballots or warriors smacking their shields in acclamation.

A *break* can be satisfying, such as breaking your fast, breaking bread together, breaking wind, and performing your civic duty by breaking a pot to cast a vote.

Coffee

An often-told myth attributes the discovery of coffee to goats. One day, a trip of goats didn't respond to the goatherd's call, and when he finally found them on the mountainside, they were dancing on their hind legs. Turns out they had dined on the red berries of a coffeebush. The goatherd nibbled too, then kicked up his heels and decided they were right to get down and party.

For millions around the word, coffee is now the pick-me-upper of choice. It's the perfect potable, the first thing on the agenda, the *sine qua non* ("essential need") before you set out for the day. How did that immense popularity come to be?

Coffee very likely originated in Ethiopia (Abyssinia) sometime before 1000 CE. Fast-forward to the sixteenth  century, and coffee had spread throughout the Arab world. It had become a major export of the Ottoman Turks and, soon after, of Dutch traders. The word *coffee* enters the English language at this point (the first recorded instance of the word was in 1598), borrowed from the Dutch word *koffie*. The Dutch word in turn had come from Turkish *kahveh*, which came from Arabic *qahwa*, which may go back to an Arab word meaning "wine" and, before that, "to have no appetite." Caffeine may suppress appetite for some, but only briefly.

Besides bringing coffee to England, the Dutch managed to cultivate a few coffee seedlings, possibly by smuggling beans out of Yemen; they brought these to Java and Sri Lanka, where they thrived (both the seedlings and the Dutch traders). Spanish, Portuguese, and French colonialists also spread coffee around the world, establishing plantations in Guatemala, Brazil, Haiti, Martinique, and other parts of South America and the Caribbean. A partial answer to the question about coffee's worldwide popularity is *colonialism*—the practice of gaining control over another country and exploiting it for political and economic ends—which happened in virtually all the places where coffee traders established plantations. Colonialism also accounts to a great extent for the global spread of English and for many borrowed words in its vocabulary. In these early days of coffee trading and cultivating, however, the British weren't yet big players (but see *tea* and *sugar,* pp. 36, 42).

Since at least the early fifteenth century, coffee has been both praised and condemned, both consumed and banned, by religious leaders of different faiths as well as by secular authorities. Perhaps because coffee was so wildly popular, it aroused suspicion, but the early objections often concerned *where* coffee was drunk rather than how the brew itself might affect the drinker. There were complaints, of course, about the drink's side effects: An English pamphlet supposedly written by women in 1674 said coffee "eunuched" their husbands. But that claim didn't seem to dampen anyone's enthusiasm for coffee, which was also touted as medicinal, its proponents saying it dispelled fumes and giddiness from the head and cured everything from dropsy to scurvy.

The real trouble with coffee, according to many authorities, was the coffeehouse.

Coffeehouses annoyed leaders and pleased the populace. Probably originating in fifteenth-century Mecca, they flourished in the Ottoman Empire of the sixteenth century and spread quickly to the Western world. These noisy, exciting places were full of would-be wits, books, journals, pipes (and, in some places, hoo-kahs), and danger from the constant flames under boiling pots of water. Leaders had reason to be concerned about these gathering places — the denizens in at least one coffeehouse did foment revolution (see p. 31, about Adams and Revere in the Green Dragon).

In England and France, coffeehouses were deemed unsuitable for women, but women found a way in. Émilie du Châtelet, an eighteenth-century French mathematician and philosopher, was kicked out of the Café Gradot in Paris, but after changing into men's clothes, she had no trouble crossing the threshold. She challenged gender norms in many ways, pursuing science, extramarital love, and the gambling table. She and Voltaire collaborated on a partial French translation of Newton's *Principia*. He got the credit. She went on to write a fuller translation with more attention to the math.

Off the Menu: Coffee with Hubby on the Side

Take a break and listen to Bach's "Coffee Cantata" (circa 1732), a comic mini-opera about a young, vivacious, coffee-loving woman and her disapproving father. He tries to put the kibosh on her caffeinated pleasures, threatening not to find her a husband if she doesn't stop drinking coffee. But she outwits her father and gets what she wants – a hubby and a cuppa joe – singing beautifully throughout her ordeal. And she's not alone in her desires. Her final aria declares that women will always stick together and remain "coffee-sisters."

The cantata satirizes the eighteenth-century hysteria over coffee. Even Frederick the Great seemed crazed because of coffee, maybe because he consumed eight cups in the morning and a pot in the afternoon. But he feared that the excessive imports would destroy the Prussian economy, so he (supposedly) employed undercover smellers to roam the streets and sniff out illegal coffee-bean roasters. But to no avail. Coffee drinking and coffeehouses became more popular than ever.

Coffeehouses have played a role in the increasing popularity of coffee in North America. One of the earliest coffeehouses in the colonies was Boston's Green Dragon Tavern (at the time, there was little distinction between a coffeehouse and a tavern), which operated from 1697 to 1832. Samuel Adams, Paul Revere, and others met there to cook up a rebellion. American colonists increased their coffee consumption after the Boston Tea Party, when tea drinking became unpatriotic. Coffee soon became as crazily popular in the United States as it was in Europe.

Undercover coffee sniffer

In the mid-twentieth century, the coffee hangouts of the Lower East Side in Manhattan lacked the splendor, chandeliers, and high ceilings of the grand cafés of Venice and Paris, but they thrived, attracting those who were thirsty for conversation about books and ideas. They appealed especially to counterculture poets and musicians—mocha with a little Dylan on the side or the Ink Spots singing "Java Jive." Coffeehouses of the 2020s, where latte sippers often talk to someone on a screen rather than in the room, provide a space to be both focused and relaxed, surrounded by others but private, with no alcohol and generally no rowdiness. Who knows what great intellectual ideas and romances are brewing? Not to mention the good things coffee drinkers might (emphasis on *might*) be doing for their health. Coffee might (or might not) have all sorts of benefits, like reducing the risks of stroke and dementia.

Here are some of coffee's many names:

Java is short for java coffee, the dark rich brew from the island of Java in the Malay Archipelago, now part of Indonesia.

Mocha takes its name from the city of al-Mukhā in Yemen on the Red Sea. In the eighteenth century, coffee was shipped from this port, so the English word *mocha,* like *java,* is a *toponym,* a word derived from a place. *Mocha,* again like the word *java,* used to mean "coffee" in a general sense as well as coffee from a particular place, but *mocha* is now associated with chocolate-flavored coffee.

If *java* and *mocha* were once at the fine end of the coffee spectrum, a cup of mud has always been at the other end. Somewhere in the middle is a cup of joe. How *joe* came to mean "coffee" is uncertain, but it might have come from the 1930s U.S. military slang term *GI Joe* (*GI,* an abbreviation for "government issue," and *Joe,* meaning "any private soldier"). Whether government-issue coffee was more like mud or fine java, it became known as *joe,* the drinker's name being transferred to the drink. *Joe* was also a term in civilian slang for "average guy," which reinforced the idea of joe as the drink of the common man (and woman?).

Popular specialty coffees, when you don't want plain joe:

Espresso is Italian for "pressed out" — coffee made by forcing steam through coffee grounds.

Cappuccino comes from the Latin for an order of friars, *Ordo Fratrum Minorum Capuccinorum.* The informal Italian word for a member of the order is *cappuccino,* from the *cappucio* ("hood") that was part of the habit worn by these friars. Because the habit resembles the color of coffee made with frothed milk, the drink became known as *cappuccino.*

Latte is espresso and steamed milk, milkier than a cappuccino, from the Italian word for "milk."

If your espresso isn't making quite the right impression on your guests, you might correct the situation by adding a shot of grappa. The drink is now a *caffè corretto* (Italian for "corrected coffee"). Grappa is brandy made from the skin, pits, stalks, and any other residue of grapes after they've been pressed in winemaking (*grappa* is from the Italian for "grape stalk," although the word is ultimately of Germanic origin).

Café de olla is a traditional Mexican coffee now popular in the United States and elsewhere. The drink, from the Spanish for "pot coffee," gets its earthy flavor from the clay pot (*olla*) it's made in and its sweet, spicy flavor from raw cane sugar (known as *piloncillo*) and a dash of cinnamon.

Turkish coffee is still made today the way it has been for centuries: in a long-handled copper pot called a *cezve* or *ibrik*. The strong black coffee with a little froth on top is usually sweetened (but if you prefer no sugar, you can order it *sade*, "simple" in Turkish).

For *affogato* and *Irish coffee*, see pp. 192 and 194.

Nowadays, we hear a lot about fair-trade coffee—from an industry whose history is replete with exploitation. When sourcing their coffee, fair-trade companies consider farms' working conditions and wages as well as environmental issues like deforestation. Some critics say it's only *greenwashing,* a word coined in the 1980s that means using environmental and ethical concerns as a cover for corporate practices that don't benefit the farmer.

Tea

The word *tea* came into the English language in the mid-seventeenth century. The Dutch were apparently the first to introduce tea to Europe, bringing it from Malaysia. The word, however, is ultimately Chinese (Min dialect *te*, related to Mandarin *chá*). By the mid-eighteenth century, tea surpassed coffee in popularity in Britain, and this surge in tea drinking coincided with Great Britain exerting control over much of Southeast Asia and India.

This takeover was largely the work of the British East India Company. Formed in England in 1599 to develop trade in tea, silk, cotton, indigo dye, spices, and other desirables, including, eventually, **opium** (see p. 49), the East India Company grew into a militarized corporation with some 250,000 troops; its charter gave it the right to wage war and collect taxes. It pillaged and violently subjugated virtually an entire subcontinent, and the company ruled there until the British monarchy took over in 1858.

One result of the company's longtime oppressive presence in the East was the enrichment of the English lexicon. Many words have come into English from Hindi and Urdu (closely related languages spoken in India, Pakistan, and elsewhere). They include *bungalow,* from Hindi for "a cottage built for Westerners in Bengal"; *pajamas,* from Urdu and Persian for "leg clothing"; *loot,* from Hindi slang for "plunder"; and many food terms, such as **chutney,** from Hindi *chattni,* "to lick," and **punch,** Hindi *panch,* from Sanskrit *pañca,* meaning "five" (referring to the number of ingredients; see p. 202). Besides expanding the English lexicon, British colonialism in the East filled Western pantries with tea. Here are a few kinds:

Pekoe is a black tea (oxidized, not fermented); its leaves are picked young, when they are covered with white down, as reflected in the Chinese name *pek,* "white," and *ho,* "down." The leaves are then oxidized—exposed to air to dry and darken, increasing aroma and flavor.

The leaves of *Lapsang souchong* are dried over burning pine, which imparts a smoky flavor to this black tea from China. *Lapsang* is apparently a coined term, although we don't know who coined it. The word *souchong* comes from Chinese *siú,* "small," and *chúng,* "sort."

Oolong, literally "black dragon" in Chinese, is a semi-oxidized tea — more oxidized than green tea, but less so than black. *Matcha* is powdered green tea leaves, used as flavoring in desserts as well as for making tea. Via Japanese, the word is ultimately from Chinese *mat,* "to rub or daub," and *cha,* "tea." *Chanoyu,* from Japanese for "hot water for tea," is the ceremony of preparing and drinking matcha.

Earl Grey is the Western name for a black tea from China (originally keemun was used, but other varieties have been employed since then) flavored with bergamot, an oil extracted from certain Seville oranges. Earl Grey is probably named after the second Earl Grey of England (1764–1845) and thus is an eponym, or a noun named after a person, if indeed the earl had much to do with this tea. He might not have wanted his name attached to the tea because adding bergamot was for a time considered a disreputable practice. But the tea became very popular in England, and his name stuck. The word *bergamot* probably comes from the northern Italian province of Bergamo and thus is a toponym.

Darjeeling is also a toponym, named after the mountainous area in northeastern India where the tea grows. Though called a black tea, it is sometimes a mixture of green and oolong leaves with a flavor often described as floral. (For other food terms named after people and places, see chapter 3.)

Chai is Indian tea made by boiling the tea leaves with milk, sugar, and **cardamom.** The word is from Chinese (Mandarin dialect) *chá*. *Cardamom* is from Greek (via French and Latin) *kardamon*, "cress," and *amōmon*, "a spice plant." Some also like to add nutmeg to their mug of chai. *Nutmeg* is related to the word *musk*, both words descending from the same Sanskrit root meaning "scrotum." Perhaps it isn't surprising, given the look of nutmeg, that it's slang for "balls" and is considered by many to be an aphrodisiac. *To nutmeg* is also slang for kicking a soccer ball between someone's legs. But nutmeg has a dark side — it can be toxic, even fatal, in high doses. Thankfully it's all joy when served in small amounts. When sprinkled on oatmeal or into chai or added to cookies and other baked goods, nutmeg has many benefits. It's rich in antioxidants; it's anti-inflammatory and mildly antibacterial; and it tastes earthy and sweet.

Kombucha is tea made from kelp (from Japanese *kobu*, "seaweed," and *cha*, "tea"). But the term in English has come to mean a rather different beverage: green or black tea that has been sweetened with sugar and fermented with SCOBY, an acronym for "symbiotic culture of bacteria and yeast." Like a starter for making sourdough bread, SCOBY can be taken from a previous batch — called a *mushroom* or a *mother* — to create a new culture. Fermented kombucha contains nutrients including B_6, B_{12}, and thiamine, and because it is made with live cultures, many consider it a probiotic (from *pro*, "for," and Greek *bios*, "life"). This fermented drink probably originated in northeastern China; modern Chinese terms for it include *haipao,* "stomach treasure," and *hongchajun,* "red tea bacteria." For reasons that are not clear, English speakers in the twentieth century adopted the Japanese word *kombucha* to designate tea made with SCOBY, not kelp.

If your SCOBY turns into a leathery-looking lump, no problem — you can wear it. When dried, SCOBY becomes microbial cellulose that can be molded to create seamless clothes. Questions remain. For example, what about comfort? And can you eat your shirt when you're tired of wearing it? (Perhaps, but it won't do you much good. Humans can't digest cellulose.)

Lahpet is a form of fermented tea eaten as a vegetable in Myanmar. Fermented teas are compressed and sold in various shapes, including logs, cakes, bricks, bowls, and bird's nests. In Korea, the pressed tea called ***doncha*** ("money tea") is shaped like coins.

Boba tea is a popular frothy cold drink originating in Taiwan in the 1980s; boba teashops quickly sprang up in the western United States and elsewhere. Made with sweetened tea, creamer or condensed milk, and chewy tapioca balls and usually shaken with ice and various syrups and flavors, *boba* comes from Cantonese dialect *bō ba,* meaning "bubble tea."

Tapioca, an essential ingredient in boba, is flour made from cassava roots. *Tapioca* comes from *tipioca,* "to squeeze out residue," a word from the Tupi-Guarani languages spoken in Brazil. Cassava is a plant widely cultivated in the West Indies and in Africa for its fleshy tuberous roots. The word *cassava* comes from Taino, a language of the Caribbean. *Boba* thus leads us from one continent to another, etymologically speaking.

The word *tea* appears in hundreds of compound terms — *tea ceremony, tea cozy, tea dance, teatime, tea towel,* and on and on. As slang, *tea* has meant "urine," "alcohol," "marijuana," and, more recently, "gossip" (one might ask a friend with big news to "spill the tea"). *Tea* also has an array of sexual meanings, as evidenced by the online Urban Dictionary.

Another linguistic consequence of British colonialism was the discovery, or acknowledgment, especially on the part of Western linguists, that Hindi and Urdu were related to English and most European languages through a common ancestor, Proto-Indo-European (referred to in this book without the prefix *Proto*). The people who spoke this language lived in the steppe region north of the Black Sea but began to disperse more than fifty-five hundred years ago, some groups migrating to the east, going as far as India, and some to the west. English's ancestors, once thought to be only German, French, and other European languages, included Farsi (or Persian), spoken in Iran, parts of Afghanistan, and elsewhere; Romani, the language of the Roma people; and Hindi and Urdu. It became clear why English words like *egg, fish, mead, meat, sweet, raw,* and *cook* were similar in many of these cousin languages: they all descended from the same mother tongue.

Sugar

Can you imagine a time before sugar?

Sugar wasn't in use until after the eleventh century, which explains why Old English had no word for it. Honey and fruit were virtually the only sweeteners that existed until more than a century after the Norman Conquest of 1066. By the thirteenth century, some of the rich French-speaking people in England had managed to get hold of sugar through trade connections, and soon the word *sugar* was adopted into Middle English—from French *sukere,* which in turn comes from Italian *zucchero,* which comes from (perhaps via Latin) the Arabic *sukkar.*

Only a few people could afford this desirable and expensive commodity, as costly as cloves, ginger, pepper, musk, and pearls.

(Queen Elizabeth, who had the money and means to get sugarcane, loved to suck on it and had black teeth because of it.) Better mills, irrigation, and steam engines helped reduce sugar's production costs and increase profits, but it was the sugar beet (as the name suggests, a kind of beet from which sugar is extracted), cultivated in nineteenth-century Prussia, that made sugar more affordable and widely available. The price of sugar went down, and consumption of it went up.

Way, way up. Today, the average American consumes about fifty-seven pounds of added sugars (that is, sugars or syrups added to processed food) a year. A jaw-dropping amount.

The history of sugar (and coffee) is also the history of plantations and, thus, slavery. The word *plantation* came from Latin into English in the fifteenth century; at the time it meant something "founded," such as an institution, or "implanted," such as an idea or belief. By the early seventeenth century, *plantation* meant "an estate, especially one in a British colony, where sugar, tobacco, and cotton are grown." Grown by whom? Enslaved workers. From 1619 until 1807, when the U.S. Congress abolished the slave trade, some twelve million Africans were brought to the Americas, mostly to the United States and the Caribbean, to work on plantations, which were essentially enslavement camps. *Plantation* can now mean any institution built on inequality.

A word like *plantation* shows us how language is inseparable from history and politics, as the cultivation of some foods was hugely profitable for a few but calamitous and deadly for millions.

Cream

Cream has a combination of secular and sacred history wrapped up in its etymology. The word was borrowed into Middle English from Old French *crème* (or *craime* or *cresme*), which itself was a blending of late Latin *cramum,* "cream," and ecclesiastical Latin *chrisma,* "chrism." *Chrism* is a mixture of oil and balsam used in baptism and other religious rites. (Besides referring to this holy oil, the word *cream* also referred to the fatty liquid that rises to the top of milk.) As a verb, *to cream* meant to apply the holy oil. A priest would cream it or dab it on a person's forehead, breast, hands, and so forth as part of sacramental rites and part of a monarch's coronation. To cream a monarch was a sacred event.

Creaming a monarch in the modern sense of that term—"to beat up"—could get a person in royal trouble. In bygone days, were you to make such an error, it might have been a Beefeater—a monarch's guard or a warder of the Tower of London—who would lock you in the tower. Today, however, the Beefeater's duties are largely ceremonial. *Beefeater* comes from a derogatory seventeenth-century term for a "well-fed servant." Whether or not the word is still derogatory (probably not), it's definitely shorter than the official designation: the Yeomen Warders of Her Majesty's Royal Palace and Fortress the Tower of London, and Members of the Sovereign's Body Guard of the Yeoman Guard Extraordinary.

Before the word *cream* arrived, speakers who wanted to refer to anointing with holy oil used the Old English word *smerian,* "to smear." This old word continued to be, even when the newer words *cream* and *anoint* (from Greek *khriein,* "to anoint") came along. But over the centuries, *smear* and *cream* lost their solemn quality. Nowadays, you might *cream* an opponent on the soccer field or *smear* a political opponent in the press. In the twenty-first century, *smear* has moved into the domain of rock climbing. It means rubbing the sole of your shoe against the rock surface to produce friction and gain purchase.

Besides putting cream and sugar in coffee, people have added spices, such as cinnamon (see *café de olla,* p. 35), and aromatics, like **ambergris.** From Old French *ambre gris,* or "gray amber" (not to be confused with the resin called amber), ambergris is a waxy glob formed in a sperm whale's intestines from indigestible squid beaks (ouch) and excreted, although some say it's formed in the stomach and puked up. Some of these globs are huge. Either way, puked or pooped, not an auspicious origin for an aromatic.

Apparently, it does smell good — not right away, but after considerable tossing around in the sea. Used in perfume manufacture, this floating commodity was fished out of the sea or cut out of a harpooned whale or washed up onto the shore, in which case lucky beachcombers could plop it in their coffee or in their claret, according to Melville's *Moby-Dick,* or fatten their wallets by selling it (although that is now illegal). Melville devoted an entire chapter (rather funny, if you're into olfactory humor) to this whale-gut desideratum.

Even Lucifer in Milton's *Paradise Regained* recognized the power of ambergris. When trying to tempt Jesus, who was fasting in the wilderness, Lucifer conjured up a richly spread table piled high with meat and fowl prepared in multiple ways — in pastry, on a spit, boiled, steamed with ambergris. The feast also included fish, wine, handsome young men and women to serve, and wonderful music.

All very tempting, but no go. Lucifer had had better luck with the apple and Eve.

Off the Menu: Fabric

Seersucker sounds like candy on a stick. Perhaps it also looks good enough to eat. The word *seersucker* comes from Hindi *śīrśakar,* from earlier Persian *šir o šakar,*

meaning "milk and sugar." The phrase probably refers to the fabric's alternating (milky) smooth and (sugary) bumpy stripes. The bumps come from a weaving process that produces puckering; these sugary-bumpy puckers keep the cloth from sticking to the skin and help circulate air.

British traders imported the striped linen or cotton fabric along with the word *seersucker* in the early eighteenth century, one of the many words that entered English as a result of the British colonialist period in India. In the United States, *seersucker* was associated with sturdy work clothes well into the twentieth century. Nevertheless, the "milk and sugar" fabric has been the fashion choice of anyone wanting to be cool.

Juice

Anyone for apple ooze? If you wanted a refreshing goblet of *juice* in Anglo-Saxon times, you might have asked for *wōs*, the Old English word meaning "juice, sap" from which we get *ooze;* not so appetizing to a modern ear. The word *juice* wasn't available until the thirteenth century, when English speakers borrowed it from the French. It's ultimately from Latin *jūs,* meaning "broth, sauce, or liquid of animal or plant."

Some words have a juicy past:

Opium comes from Greek *opos,* meaning "juice." For many thousands of years, opium has been valued for the pain relief, not to mention euphoria, it brings, as well as for other real and supposed medical benefits (as a cure for headache, insomnia, diarrhea, melancholia, menstrual cramps, and on and on). The origin of this stupendous drug is humble: poppies in the field. Long before scientists in a lab created synthetic opioids, the ancient Sumerians and others were harvesting opium. They sliced open the unripened seedpod of the poppy to catch its oozing, opium-rich latex (the fluid or juice of a plant). This juice today gives us morphine, heroin, codeine, and other opiates. Given the modern opioid crisis, perhaps it's good to keep in mind the old name for this plant juice — tear(s) of the poppy. That's also the literal meaning of a scientific name for opium, *Lachryma papaveris.*

Succulent comes from Latin *succus,* "juicy." As a noun, it refers to a kind of plant that needs little water, like a cactus. But as an adjective, *succulent* can mean "tender and tasty." *Succulent* seems like a contranym, a word with opposite meanings, in this case both "dry" and "juicy." The cactus plant is dry in that it's a *xerophyte,* from Greek *xēros*, "dry," and *-phyte*, "plant," but the fleshy leaves of a succulent are in fact juicy, because they store water.

Succulent is part of a big family of words that derive from the Indo-European root *seuə-*, "to take in liquid." *Sip, sop, sup,* and *suck* are some of *succulent's* cognates, or cousin words. The surprising cousin is **prosciutto.** How does a dried meat fit in this family of sippers? In this case, the liquid is not taken in but removed. *Prosciutto* is an altered form of *asciutto*, "dried," its derivation going back to Latin *exsūctus*, "sucked out."

Another juicy word, etymologically speaking, is *zaftig*, meaning "buxom"; it comes from Yiddish *zaftik*, meaning "juicy." How did *juicy* come to mean "buxom"? There's no easy answer to that. The evolution of the word *buxom* is a curious case of semantic change and is worth a little meandering before we come back to *zaftig*. *Buxom* comes from Old English *bugan*, "to bow or bend," combined with the adjective-forming suffix *-sum*. *Buxom* originally meant "pliant" and "obedient," and it could refer to any person, regardless of gender. Over the centuries, *buxom* came to mean "amiable," then "jolly, well-favored, and plump." This physical sense of *buxom*, rather than the earlier moral sense, came to be used primarily in reference to women. The word now means having a "curvy, ample, or zaftig figure."

Bread

Bread is a miracle of transformation. Bread-like food made from wild, undomesticated grasses appeared around 14,000 BCE, predating agriculture by some four thousand years. But this food, perhaps a kind of flatbread or cooked porridge, did not become a staple until grain was cultivated. At some point in the long history of bread, whether before or after domesticating grain, someone learned to control and grow yeast (yeasts are found naturally in soil and on plant surfaces) and added it to the flour made from grinding grain. And—miracle of miracles—leavened flour rose up in glory.

For some, the joy of bread comes from the swollen dough, because it invites kneading—punching and turning, pushing with the heel of your hand, turning and pushing, and finally shaping the dough into a big belly, a loaf, or a long stick. For others, the joy comes from the smell as the bread bakes or from the taste and texture of the baked loaf—the crispy crust and the slightly tangy, soft but chewy inside.

Bakers are *lords* and *ladies,* in an old sense. A *lord* was, etymologically, "loaf warden," from Old English *hlāford,* formed from *hlāf,* "loaf," combined with *weard,* "ward or guard." And a *lady* was "loaf kneader," from *hlǣfdīge,* "loaf," combined with *dige,* "knead." Regardless of what these etymologies imply about gender and the division of labor in early Germanic times, they suggest the cultural centrality of bread.

Today, there's *bread* in the slang sense of money in your wallet. But in its primary sense, *bread* (from Old English *brēad*) has hardly changed over the centuries. One aspect of bread that does change is its shape. It might be a long and narrow **baguette,** a word that comes ultimately from Latin *baculum,* "a staff." In French, *baguette* can mean "stick" or "wand," and if you read Harry Potter in a French translation, you'll find him working his magic by waving a *baguette.*

Another breadbox might contain a thickish, flat, rectangular *ciabatta,* which means "slipper" in Italian (but for what kind of foot?). Or perhaps the breadbox has teardrop-shaped *naan* (from Urdu and Persian *nān*) or flat and oval *ingera* (from Amharic, spoken in Eritrea and Ethiopia). Some bread is braided, like *challah* (from Hebrew *challah*). And the round, doughnut-shaped *bagel* comes from Yiddish *beygel,* which in turn is possibly from a German word meaning "ring" or "bracelet."

Other bready words:

Brew is probably a cousin of *bread,* both descendants of the Indo-European root *bhreuə,* "to boil, bubble." Brewing ale and making bread both involve knowledge of different kinds of yeast and the art of controlling fermentation. (See pp. 51, 103–104.)

A *bribe,* from Old French *briber,* was originally a bit of bread or other food given to a beggar. It could also mean an improper inducement or extortion — in other words, a *bribe* in the modern sense of the word.

Sop, from Old English *soppian,* "to dip bread in wine or other liquid," also meant a bribe in the form of food given to pacify. But sops were not always bribes; they could simply be delicious treats, like the ones enjoyed by Chaucer's Merchant in the *Canterbury Tales.* This rich guy loved sex and sops "in the morn." (For a good time, read these tales!)

Off the Menu: Alms

A *bribe* wasn't always extortion. In the sense of "piece of bread," a bribe given to beggars in medieval times could be *alms* or a charitable offering (from Old English *ael-mysse*, borrowed via Latin from Greek *eleēmosunē*, meaning "compassion"). Words relating to *alms* include *alma mater* (Latin for "nurturing mother") and *alumni* and *alumnae* ("foster sons" and "foster daughters") — those whose hungry minds were nourished well enough to leave the alma mater.

Fruit

How can fruit be anything but delightful? It's sweet, nutritious, and delicious. It also invites symbolic meanings that are often contradictory. If an apple is the forbidden fruit in Eden, it is both sinful and a source of knowledge. The seeds of the pomegranate eaten by Persephone, goddess of spring growth, hold her in the underworld, but she returns to the world of the living every spring. Even the history of the word *fruit* contains seeming contradictions.

Fruit comes from Latin *fruī,* "to enjoy," but *fruī* has also given us *frugal,* a word that may put a damper on enjoyment.

Here are some enjoyable fruit-filled word histories:

Apple comes from Old English *æppel.* Besides its primary meaning as a "round fruit with crisp flesh," the word has referred to the fruit eaten by Adam and Eve in the Garden of Eden. The forbidden fruit is not actually named in Genesis, but some Jewish commentators on the Torah said it was the fig, and Michelangelo made it figlike on the Sistine Chapel ceiling; a thirteenth-century translator of the Spanish Jewish philosopher Maimonides declared it was the banana, and early Christian theologians writing in Latin opted for an apple. The Latin word for *apple, mālum,* gave them the occasion to exploit its potential for punning: *malum* can also mean "evil."

Avocado comes from *ahuacatl* in the Nahuatl language, spoken in southern Mexico and Central America. Besides referring to the fruit, *ahuacatl* can mean "testicle," and there has been considerable debate as to which meaning came first.

Avocado came into English from the Spanish *aguacate,* a form of *ahuacatl,* influenced by the Spanish word *avocado* (modern *abogado*), "advocate, lawyer." The connection between the fruit and the lawyer is only the similarity in sound. **Guacamole** also comes via Spanish from Nahuatl *ahuacatl,* "avocado, testicle," and *molli,* "sauce."

The word *banana* came into English in the sixteenth century via Portuguese or Spanish from Wolof, an Atlantic-Congo language, or Mande, a branch of the Niger-Congo family of languages. The banana has a notable old European botanical name, *Musa sapientum,* "fruit of the wise men." *Mūsa* means "muse" in classical Latin, but in Old French and medieval Latin, *musa* also meant "banana" and, more generally, "fruit." It's a loanword from Arabic *mawz* or Turkish *muz,* meaning "banana." It's not surprising that the eighteenth-century botanist Carl Linnaeus, the father of taxonomy, named the genus to which the banana belonged *Musa.*

But why name the species *sapientum*, "of the wise men"? Speculation abounds and includes the notion that bananas were the fruit eaten by wise men in India or the fruit from the tree in the Garden of Eden called "the tree of the knowledge of good and evil." In other words, the forbidden fruit. Whatever the reason for the designation, *Musa sapientum* is being superseded by the less thought-provoking, more prosaic term *Musa acuminata,* "pointed or tapering fruit."

Far from being wise, if you *go bananas,* you've gone crazy. But if you're *top banana,* you're important. The latter expression originally meant "the top comedian in a vaudeville show," probably because of a skit involving a banana.

Coconut comes from sixteenth-century Spanish and Portuguese *coco* combined with *nut. Coco* means "grinning face"; apparently it was applied because the holes at the base of the coconut suggest a smile. The *snoot* in Dutch *kokosnoot* and the *snot* in Swedish *kokosnöt* have nothing to do with snoot or snot; *kokosnoot* and *kokosnöt* both mean "coconut." When rumors ran wild in the ether in the early 2000s that falling coconuts posed a serious risk to humans, the coconut became known as "the killer fruit." But statistics suggest that's a little on the nutso side, and the rumormongers were probably uninformed urbanites.

Grapefruit originated in Barbados as a hybrid of orange and pomelo, both of which were introduced into the West Indies from

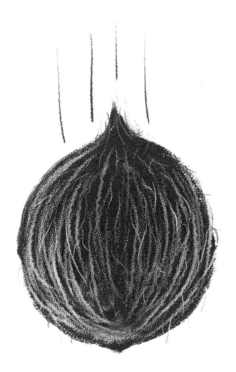

Asia. The fruit has been known by many names, including *shaddock,* from Captain Shaddock, who might have introduced the pomelo into Jamaica, and *citrus of paradise,* which is now reflected in its botanical name, *Citrus x paradisi.* A common explanation — which requires a stretch of the imagination — for the name **grapefruit** is that the fruit grows in clusters, like grapes. Really big grapes.

The *musk* in **muskmelon** comes via Latin and Persian, from

Sanskrit *muska,* "scrotum," because of the similarity in shape between the melon and the male deer's sac in which musk is made. (Try not to think about that next time you're scooping melon balls.) **Melon** is a contraction of Latin *mēlopepō,* from Greek *mēlon,* "apple," and *pepōn,* "gourd."

Honeydew is one of relatively few food words in these pages not borrowed from another language. It's an example of a new word formed within Old English by compounding; in this case, *hunig,* "honey," and *dēaw,* "dew." But in Old English, the word *hunigdēaw* did not refer to a melon. It was a synonym of *mildēaw,* Old English for "mildew." The *mil* in *mildēaw* meant "honey," but this honey as well as the honey in *hunigdēaw* referred to a substance secreted on plants by aphids. The *dew* of *mildēaw* and *hunigdēaw* came from the belief that the sticky aphid substance dropped from the sky, like dew. Not until the twentieth century did the word *honeydew* come to mean a particular kind of melon with green flesh, and *honeydew* still retains the meaning of "sticky aphid secretion."

Would you prefer a melon with no connection to bugs? How about to wolves? **Cantaloupe,** a variety of muskmelon, is a toponym, or a word named for a place. It comes from Cantalupo (literally, "singing or howling wolf"), a papal country seat outside Rome, although the melon itself may have originated in Armenia. Legend has it that Pope Paul II loved melons (as well as fancy ecclesiastical clothing, art, and collecting antiques), and that he died from eating two melons at one sitting. Death by melon is hard to swallow, unless the melons were covered in aphid goo and the howling wolves were heart-stoppingly scary. (For popes, wine, and lettuce, see p. 7.)

The etymology of *grape* suggests how the fruit was harvested. *Grape* comes from Old French *grape* and, earlier, *grapper,* "to gather with a hook."

Lemon and *lime* both come ultimately from Arabic *limun,* a collective name for these fruits. Figuratively, a *lemon* is a disappointing purchase, like a new but troublesome car. But lemons also give us *zest,* energy and enthusiasm, as well as a piquant flavoring for food from the grated peel. *Zest* derives from French *zec,* referring to a membrane around a walnut kernel.

Orange trees originated in southern China, northeastern India, and Myanmar. The word *orange* came into English in the fifteenth century from French, going back to Arabic *nāranj,* ultimately from Persian *nārang.*

An interesting detail about the word *orange* (besides the fact it has no rhyme): The loss of the *n* from *nāranj* probably happened because the French or English misperceived that consonant as being part of an indefinite article, as if *nāranj* meant *une orange* ("an orange"). This linguistic process of misperceiving the boundary of a word has a name. Actually, it has an epic list of names,

including but not limited to *juncture loss, rebracketing, resegmenta-*
tion, reanalysis, and *metanalysis.*

The process of wrongly adding or omitting an *n* has occurred
many times in English: *Nickname* comes from misperceiving the
original boundaries of *an eke name* (literally, "an other name"). A
newt was originally *an ewt.* An *apron* was *a napron,* and an *umpire*
was *a noumpire.* A similar principle is at work when people say, as
they often do, "That's a whole *nother* matter."

Did the color orange exist for English speakers before the fruit
came into their lives? Most likely it did, as evidenced by the Old
English compound term *ġeolurēad,* "yellow-red." Nevertheless, the
fruit may well have inspired a new color word, *orange,* though it

took a while. The first recorded instance of *orange* clearly referring to a color appeared about a hundred years after English speakers had been eating and talking about the fruit.

The papaya is native to tropical America, eventually spreading to the Caribbean. The word **papaya** came into English in the sixteenth century via Spanish from an Arawakan language of the Caribbean. *Papaya* is also called *pawpaw* (perhaps a shortened form of *papaya*) in Australia, New Zealand, and other British Commonwealth countries.

Interesting fact: The plant is said to be *trioecious* (from Greek, "three houses"), referring to a species that can have male flowers (flowers with stamens), female flowers (flowers with pistils), and hermaphroditic flowers on separate plants. This third "house" or category consists of flowers that have both stamens and pistils. The term comes from Hermaphroditus, beautiful son of Hermes and Aphrodite. A nymph named Salmacis lusted after Hermaphroditus and prayed the two of them would be eternally united. They were joined in one body that had sexual traits of both. Neither he nor she was pleased. Today's cultivators, however, prefer hermaphrodite plants because they're self-pollinating and produce good fruit.

A rambutan is a yummy, plum-like tropical fruit. It has fine spines on its skin, reflected in its name. The word **rambutan** comes from Malay *rambūtan,* from *rambut,* "hair."

Strawberry and **raspberry** present some difficulties, etymologically speaking. The *berry* part is straightforward, but why *straw* for *strawberry*? Perhaps there's a connection with the word *strew;* maybe the strawberry runners look strewn along the ground. Likewise, the *rasp* in *raspberry* is of uncertain origin. But there's a clear enough origin of *raspberry* meaning "a rude noise." It's from nineteenth-century rhyming slang. *Raspberry tart* was a slangy way of saying *fart*. Eventually the derisive fart-like sound—made by putting tongue between lips and blowing—came to be called a *raspberry.*

Cereal

Many of us love a bowl of cereal in the morning or any time of day. If we were living two thousand or so years ago, we'd thank Ceres for this toothsome food. **Cereal** is from Latin *Cereālis,* "of or pertaining to Ceres," the Roman goddess of agriculture; she was responsible for the growth of grain. *Ceres* and *cereal* derive from the Indo-European root *ker-,* meaning "to grow." The root produced many words, as if Ceres herself were nurturing it: *create, procreate, creature, creole, increase, recruit,* and more.

As noted in the introduction, coined words account for relatively few additions to English, but W. K. Kellogg, who was in the cereal business in the early twentieth century, did his Ceres-like work and increased the English lexicon by coining the trademarked word *Granola*. In the twenty-first century, *granola* is now generic and no longer refers only to cereal. It can be an adjective, usually derogatory, for a certain kind of person—someone who's flaky and nutty.

Many people like their granola in *yogurt* (from seventeenth-century Turkish *yogurt,* meaning "fermented milk"), and many people like vanilla-flavored yogurt. The word **vanilla** ultimately derives from Latin *vāgīna,* meaning "sheath or scabbard," supposedly because of the shape of the pod (yes, a head-scratcher).

Other delicious cereal grains often eaten for breakfast:

Pone, unleavened bread or doughy cake made with maize, comes from Algonquian *apones, appoans,* "bread." Also from Algonquian, *hominy* (*uskatahomen*) are coarsely ground corn kernels boiled in water or milk. Many First Nations, including the Cherokee, Chickasaw, Choctaw, Creek, and Seminole, cultivated maize; they soaked it in lime or ash in a process called *nixtamalization* (from Nahuatl *nextli,* "ashes," and *tamalli,* "corn dough"). This process made grinding the corn easier and improved flavor and nutrition.

Grits are coarsely ground corn kernels cooked in water or milk—tasty cornmeal, and a far cry from dust, despite the word's history (from Old English *grytte,* meaning "bran or mill dust"). **Hush puppies,** another cornmeal treat, have a crunchy deep-fried

Hominy

outside and a corn-and-onion-flavored inside. The traditional explanation for the name *hush puppies* involves hunters or fishermen battering and frying their catch and throwing some cornmeal mixture to the dogs to hush them. It probably worked, though as etymology goes, it's more fanciful than factual.

Other kinds of fried dough are sweetened, like traditional Jamaican **beignets,** from French archaic *buyne,* meaning "hump" or "bump." In Jamaica, lightly sweetened cornmeal fritters are sometimes called **festivals,** and in the United States and elsewhere, beignets are sometimes called **nun's farts,** from French *pets de*

Hush puppies

nonne. Those who are too fastidious to order a *nun's fart* might prefer the euphemistic **nun's puffs** (or stick with *beignets*).

Off the Menu: Yummy Plunder

If you want a **Danish** for breakfast and you're in Denmark, what do you ask for? *Wienerbrød,* or Vienna bread, because according to tradition, Austrian bakers invented the Danish and brought it to Denmark. At the Café Central in Vienna, what do you order? *Kopenhagen Plunder.* But no need for a loot bag or beefy escort, because you're not demanding booty. The German word *plunder* can mean "loot" and "the spoils of pillaging," as well as "stuff," like junk in the attic. But an old meaning of the German verb *plundern* may have been "to rise," and in the Austrian world of baking, *plunder* has come to mean pastry.

Eggs

Pity the fifteenth-century English merchant whose departure by ship was delayed. With time to kill, he wandered around, worked up an appetite, found a tavern, and asked for *eggys*. The goodwife who waited on him said she didn't speak French. The merchant said he didn't speak French either, just bring him some *eggys*. Someone else in the tavern piped up: *Eyren;* that man wants *eyren*. The goodwife finally understood and cooked some eggs.

Eyren (singular *ei*) came from Old English, and *eggys* (singular *æg*) came from Old Norse, borrowed early into English. For centuries both words coexisted in English, and the printer who recounted the story about *eggys* and *eyren* lamented having to be an arbiter of the language, deciding which particular words to print when people spoke different dialects and which spellings to use at a time when spelling wasn't standardized. Spelling did become fairly standardized over the next two centuries, partially due to the influence of the many dictionaries compiled and printed during that time.

Today, English has absorbed so many words for eggy dishes from other languages that English speakers might not know—in a literal way—what they're asking for. They might be ordering a donkey, a knife blade, ox eyes, or Adam and Eve on a raft. Or asking to bite someone.

A breakfast *burrito,* from Spanish "little burro or donkey," comes loaded with sweet peppers, onions, cheese, sausages, hash browns if you like, and eggs, all wrapped in a tortilla. Or instead of mixing everything together, separate them: order *huevos divorciados,* or **divorced eggs.** This Mexican dish has two fried eggs, each on its own tortilla and each with a different salsa, separated by a row of refried beans.

Soufflé comes from French for "blown" and derives from the same root as *flatulent.* If you'd rather something a bit less puffed up, order an **omelet,** from Latin *lamella,* "thin plate" or "blade of a sword or knife."

A **croque-madame** is grilled cheese with ham on bread, topped with an egg. It comes from French for "crunch or bite a woman." If you'd rather "bite a man," have a **croque-monsieur,** but it lacks the egg.

Here's looking at you: A **sunny-side-up** egg is fried and not flipped over, its yolk staring at you. In many languages, a fried egg

is an "eye," as in Greek *avgá mátia,* "eggs eyes." In Japanese, it's *medama yaki,* a "cooked eyeball." In Indonesian, it's *telur mata sapi,* a "cow's eye egg," and in Czech, it's *volské oko,* "an ox eye." In German, a fried egg isn't an eye but a *spiegelei,* "a mirror egg," so it still may seem to be looking at you.

An old culinary tradition that's currently very fashionable in the United States is to put a fried egg on top of everything — rice dishes, pizza, hamburgers, maybe even oatmeal. If your food has an egg on top, the egg is *au cheval,* French for "on horseback." Similarly, in northern Mexico, eggs on steak are *huevos montados,* "riding eggs."

If you want your egg on toast with a little cheese, order a **buck rarebit,** but don't expect meat. It has no rabbit in it, even though *rarebit* derives from the word *rabbit,* and a male rabbit is called a *buck.* **Welsh rarebit,** cheese on toast without the egg, is also called *Welsh rabbit,* but it is likewise rabbit-less.

If you're in a diner and want eggs on toast, order **Adam and Eve on a raft.** Want the eggs scrambled? Say, "I'll have Adam and Eve on a raft—and wreck 'em." Like the term *sunny-side up,* the Adam and Eve lingo comes from diners, where the person who'd taken the order yelled it to the cook in the kitchen. Or at least, that's the theory. Some claim it was created to amuse customers and was never actual cook-talk, but in any case, it's all part of the noisy good vibes in the diner. As slang and lingo go, this short-order cook-talk is long-lived. It's been around for more than a hundred years.

Off the Menu: A Breakfast to Avoid

If you're trying to put together a complicated toy or install a new router, you hope the instructions are not a *dog's breakfast*—British slang for a big confusing mess.

2

Midmorning Java Break

Food Origins of Computer Jargon

```
┌─────────────────────────────────────────────────────────┐
│ ▤ □ ▤▤▤▤▤▤▤▤▤▤▤▤▤▤▤▤▤▤▤▤▤▤▤▤▤▤▤▤▤▤▤▤▤▤▤▤▤▤▤ │
│                                                           │
│                                                           │
│         DO YOU ACCEPT THAT ALL                            │
│         COOKIES ARE DELICIOUS?                            │
│                                                           │
│                                                           │
│              ┌─────────────────────┐                     │
│              │                     │                     │
│              │      ACCEPT         │                     │
│              │                     │                     │
│              └─────────────────────┘                     │
│                                                           │
└─────────────────────────────────────────────────────────┘
```

Breakfast was an hour ago, and you're already hungry again. It's not your fault. With all the food words juicing up the jargon of the internet, you're probably reminded of eating every time you turn on a digital device. Consider the evidence.

Java, a programming language created in the 1990s, may have been named because insane quantities of coffee were drunk during its development. Shortly thereafter, a scripting language that makes web pages interactive was developed. Apparently first named *Mocha,* it was renamed *JavaScript*. For non-techies eager to understand the differences between *Java* and *JavaScript,* brew strong coffee and start surfing.

A ***chip*** is a tiny square of semiconducting material that can be made into an integrated circuit. A life-altering invention, right up there with the BBQ variety.

Cookie, from Dutch *koekje,* "little cake," is now a packet of data on a computer that is created and read by website servers to identify the user and track visits to sites. It's like a cookie jar that knows where your hand has been.

Copypasta is a block of text that has been copied and spread online, something that becomes a meme. Why *pasta?* It's probably a play on the word *paste,* as in *copy and paste.*

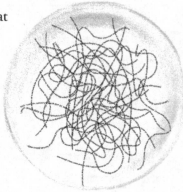

Hamburger refers to an inhabitant of Hamburg, Germany, or ground beef in a bun (see discussion of foods named after places, pp. 102–106). In the virtual world, a *hamburger* means those three parallel bars that often appear with a pulldown menu in the top right or left corner of your screen.

A *lunchbox* was an early portable computer first released in 1987 that weighed twenty pounds. Makes you wonder what was in the actual lunch box of the person who named it. Thick bread and huge hunks of cheese? That would be in keeping with the early meaning of the word **lunch**—"a lump or hunk" (see p. 87).

Menu comes from French for a "detailed list" (ultimately from Latin *minūtus,* "very small"). On a screen, as in a restaurant, a *menu* is a list of options, but no server will take your food order and deliver it to your table.

A server will, however, store data from a host so that it can be accessed across the internet. Not strictly food terms, *host* and *server* nevertheless pertain to both data and food and fit the menu here. *Host* comes from Latin *hospes,* meaning either "host" or "guest." The word *server* has a much less hospitable origin, from Latin *servus,* "slave."

The term *phishing* is also indirectly related to food. As if trying to reel in fish, scammers send e-mails purporting to be from legitimate companies in order to get people to reveal passwords, credit card numbers, and other personal info.

Off the Menu: A Watched Pot

One day in 1991 at Cambridge University, a researcher needed a cup of coffee. Battling eyestrain and foggy brain (one imagines), he trudged down the hall, up the stairs, around the corner, up another flight of stairs, and on and on to the coffeemaker that was stationed in the

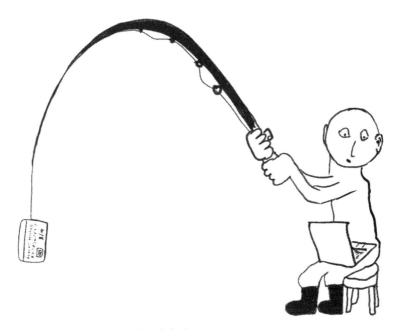

Careful what you phish for.

corridor outside the computer lab's Trojan Room. Alas, the so-called Trojan coffeepot was empty.

To guard against caffeine disappointment in the future, a couple of plucky researchers thought up a plan. They focused a camera on the pot and connected the feed to a video frame grabber in the Trojan Room, then created a program that allowed researchers to see a frequently updated image of the coffeepot. No more wasted to-ing and fro-ing to check on the coffee supply. Thus, the serendipitous but nevertheless spectacular invention of what eventually became the webcam, now used by zillions of Zoomers, FaceTimers, and other lookers every day.

The live feed remained active for a decade, and the coffeepot became so famous that when it was retired, it sold on eBay for thousands of pounds. The coffeepot is now living out its retirement in a German museum.

Feed in the cyber age isn't food but electronic information, like the scroll of an Instagram feed. The 1920s term *feedback,* meaning "return of output signal," has gone beyond the world of electronics; it is used to describe any modification of a process or system resulting from that process or system. *Feedback* is now almost synonymous with *response.*

A *bit* is a unit of data, a 0 or 1 in binary code, and a *byte* is a group of (usually) eight bits. The word *bit,* coined in the 1940s, is an abbreviation of *binary digit. Byte* was formed from the words *bit* and *bite,* with the *y* added (one speculates) to distinguish a digital byte from, say, a bite of toast. And a ***nibble*** is half a *byte.*

Like bits of food, **bread crumbs** have been recycled for the cyber age. They're still parts of a trail to follow, but a computer bread-crumb trail is especially helpful for navigating backward or up to a previous link and to find your way in a series of embedded words. For example, *etymology > food terms > computer terms from food > bread crumb.*

When some people run out of *juice,* they like to disconnect for a while, turn off devices, and take a nap. When devices run out of juice, though, they need to reconnect — to a power source.

Off the Menu: Dr. Muffet on Her Tuffet, Eating Her Quarks and Whey

Physicists often have a whimsical way with words. For example, when Dr. Murray Gell-Mann theorized the existence of certain subatomic particles, he played around with names for them like *squeak, squork,* and *kwork* before settling on **quark.** He was perusing (of all things) James Joyce's *Finnegans Wake,* a novel full of portmanteau words and multilingual puns that's notoriously difficult to read, according to some. Dr. Gell-Mann liked the line "three quarks for Muster [sic] Mark," which he interpreted as an order at a bar — Mr. Mark wants three quarts of ale. Quite an order. The Joycean "three quarks" seemed to match the threefold way that certain subatomic particles occur in nature, those particles that Dr. Gell-Mann eventually called *quarks*.

The word *quark* does have food (if not drink) in its past. *Quark* refers to a kind of cottage cheese; it comes from a German (originally Slavic) word meaning "curds." It can also mean "rubbish" or "nonsense." And here's another quirky science/food connection: A sweet treat played a role in the discovery of a new particle called the Higgs boson. Proof of the particle's existence was found in an accelerator's inner chamber, which some call a doughnut because of its shape. Perhaps helped by a ring-shaped food and a spirit of playfulness, the boson physicists, as well as quarky Gell-Mann, won a Nobel Prize.

Many explanations have been floated for a certain big tech company's logo of a bitten apple, including the notion that it refers to the forbidden fruit in the Garden of Eden. But the answer, apparently, is much less grand. Founder Steve Jobs may have been inspired by an apple orchard he worked in during his hippie days. A designer for the logo, Rob

Janoff, wanted to add the bite to show scale and thus make it clear that the fruit was an apple, not a cherry. Nothing biblical was intended. (For more about the forbidden fruit, see pp. 54, 55.)

If you think you spend a lot of time browsing, consider the *moose* (from the First Nations language Eastern Abenaki, *mos*). For hours a day, the moose browse for *browse*. *Browse* isn't just a verb; it's vegetation eaten by animals. It comes from Old French *brost,* "young shoot," probably of Germanic origin. Moose need up to fifty pounds of browse a day, hence the nonstop browsing.

Garbage collection is a feature in some programming languages (for example, Java) that frees up memory by automatically removing unneeded objects and other stored data. Nice when it's automatic and doesn't require a coin toss with your partner to see who will haul the trash down to the curb.

If a coder has written too many functions or too many lines out of order and made a disorganized tangle, it's *spaghetti* that the coder's fellow workers won't appreciate. They will have to sort through the mess.

Spam, meaning the unwanted e-mails that clutter our lives, probably derives from the tinned food called Spam, a portmanteau word coined in the 1930s from *spiced* and *ham.* The modern meaning of the word was also very likely influenced by the Monty Python sketch in which every item on the menu included Spam. In many regions around the world, including Guam, China, the Philippines, and Hawaii, the food called Spam is highly valued.

Off the Menu: Scuttlebutt at the Symposium

During your midmorning java break, you might hang around the watercooler to catch up on *scuttlebutt* — from U.S. nautical slang for "gossip," which in turn comes from the "scuttled butt" that held drinking water on a ship. A butt is a cask and a liquid measure equal to two hogsheads or 126 gallons. A precursor to a modern watercooler, a butt that's been scuttled is a cask with a hole through which the liquid is dispensed. (For more butts, see chapter 4, "Happy Hour.")

While you're sipping a bit of a butt of water with your colleagues, you might volunteer to organize a *symposium,* from the Greek for "fellow drinker." The word *symposium* has grown more sober over the centuries. Long ago it denoted a drinking party, but now it means a conference on a particular topic — presumably serious, often full of high-minded discussion and the presentation of formal papers, each speaker sipping from a plastic bottle. No scuttled butts in sight.

3
Lunch

Foods Named After People,
Places, and Body Parts

I f you eat a midday meal, do you call it *lunch?* What about *luncheon, nuncheon, noonshine,* or *nunch?* Perhaps you pause for refreshment toward the end of the morning and call this light repast *elevenses* (from *eleven,* as in eleven o'clock a.m.). If you skipped breakfast, your meal might be *brunch* (a portmanteau, or blended, word made from *breakfast* and *lunch*). Or maybe you call a midday meal *dinner* (and an evening meal *supper,* from Old French *super,* "to sup, take liquids by sipping").

Chances are, you don't say *noonshine* unless you're a big Jane Austen fan. *Noonshine,* meaning "noon light," has been around since the seventeenth century, but Austen appears to have been the first to apply it to a midday meal. Her particular use of *noonshine,* however, didn't catch on with the general public. But Austen, like others in the early nineteenth century, also called a midday meal *nuncheon* (from Middle English *noon* and *shenche,* "a cupful, a drink"). *Nuncheon* and its shortened form *nunch,* meaning "light refreshment" or "drink," had been around for centuries before Austen used it, and *nuncheon* lives on in regional varieties of English in the United States and the United Kingdom.

Which came first, *lunch* or *luncheon?* That doesn't matter to

someone about to tuck into an egg-salad sandwich, but postpran-
dially (from Latin *post,* "after," and *prandium,* "meal"), one might
give the matter some thought. *Lunch* is probably a shortened form
of *luncheon,* and *luncheon* probably derives from the English word
lump. In the earliest instances of *luncheon* and *lunch*—the sixteenth century—both words meant a "hunk," "lump," or "thick
piece" (of food) before they came to mean "a meal." *Luncheon* in
the sense of a midday meal first appeared in the written record in
the seventeenth century. *Lunch* (the meal, not the hunk) is a
Johnny-come-lately, not appearing until the nineteenth century.

One further speculation: Some argue that the sixteenth-
century Spanish word *lonja* ("slice" of food) is the source of the
English *lunch.* Could be, but *luncheon* predates *lonja* in the written
record by more than a decade. There's no definitive answer yet on
where our lunch comes from.

When the word *lunch* became popular in the 1800s, it was
sometimes considered vulgar, in the sense of low class. *Lunch* eventually became the more common term for the meal, *luncheon*
being reserved for more formal usage. The word *luncheon* has come
a long way, from "lump" of food to what may be a lavish meal.

As a verb, *lunch* is versatile. It's both intransitive ("You lunch
at noon") and transitive (taking a direct object, as in "You lunch a
client"). Sounds a tad cannibalistic. So does the expression *to eat*

someone's lunch, meaning "to defeat soundly," as in "My opponent ate my lunch on the tennis court."

To lunch can mean "to forget to do something," often used in the past tense. If a person forgot to buy bread on her way home from work, she lunched on that. She didn't do lunch, eat lunch, or lunch a friend; she was *out to lunch*—in the sense of "very inattentive."

Off the Menu: The Sound of Lunch

Lonche is an old word from Middle English, rarely used now, meaning "the sound of a soft but heavy body falling." It's also spelled *lunch*. Though the two *lunches*—the meal and the thud—are pronounced more or less the same, they are not etymologically related. (The same holds true for other homophones, like *dear* and *deer*, and *new* and *knew*, each word having a different origin.)

The word *lonche* meaning "a soft but heavy body falling" is imitative in origin, or onomatopoetic—it presumably sounds like what it means. If you listen to the sound of *lonche* (or *lunch*), does it suggest "a soft but heavy body falling"? It may indeed. The liquid *l*, the gruntlike vowel, the crunch of *nche*. Should we revive the word?

Or invent a new onomatopoetic word for the whump and sigh of someone collapsing on the couch after a midday meal?

Write your new word here: _____

_____

Eponyms

What's on the menu for lunch? A common choice is a *sandwich,* a word that comes from a person's name, in this case the eighteenth-century Earl of Sandwich. The story goes that the earl had a gambling problem, or, rather, a problem with eating while gambling. How to hold the cards and eat at the same time? And no one wants a plate cluttering up the gaming table. So he ate his meat between two slices of bread while gambling.

But long before the earl held his food in one hand and his cards in the other, people had been using bread as a convenient holder of other foods. (Consider the medieval slice of bread called a *trencher* that was used as an edible plate.) Even though the Earl of Sandwich didn't invent the thing we call a sandwich, it's named after him, so *sandwich* is indeed an eponym.

The sandwich called a *Reuben* may be named after Reuben Kulakofsky, a grocer of Nebraska. Sometime in the 1920s or '30s,

while he was playing poker, he had the inspiration to concoct a sandwich made of corned beef, Swiss cheese, sauerkraut, and Russian dressing on rye bread. (What is it with poker and eponymous sandwiches?) But the name may be based on a "Reuben's Special," made (possibly) in 1914 at Arthur Reuben's Deli in New York. In this case, the Reuben is both an eponym and, loosely speaking, a toponym (something named after a place, though it's usually a geographic feature, not a deli).

If you take the Reuben and substitute pastrami or turkey for the corned beef, coleslaw for the sauerkraut, and Thousand Island dressing for the Russian, you've got a **Rachel.** Whether there's an actual person behind the sandwich called a *Rachel* remains unknown.

Maybe you want something a bit simpler than a Rachel or a Reuben, like **pastrami** on **pumpernickel** with *lettuce, mustard, relish,* and **coleslaw.** Here's your sandwich, etymologically speaking:

Pastrami is from Yiddish, probably originally Turkish, meaning "pressed"—part of the curing process of the meat. *Pumpernickel* comes from early German *pumper,* "fart," and Nicholas, "a lout or bumpkin." *Lettuce* is from Latin *lactūca, lact-,* "milk," because of its milky juice. *Mustard* comes from Anglo-Norman, *must,* "new wine" or "juice from grapes." *Relish* is from Old French *relaisser,* "to release," from Latin *relaxāre,* "to relax," coming to mean "flavor-releasing," and *coleslaw* is from Dutch *kool,* ultimately from Latin *caulis,* "stem" or "cabbage," and *sla,* "slaw," a shortened form of Dutch *salade.*

So:

Pressed meat on farting-bumpkin slices, with milky juice, musty grape juice, relaxed condiments, and stem salad.

Yummy.

"What's in a name? That which we call a rose by any other name would smell as sweet," Juliet says when she discovers her hot

hunk Romeo is a Montague, the clan feuding with her own family, the Capulets. But *would* a rose or a lover by any other name smell as sweet? What if his name had been Romeo Pumpernickel, of the farting-bumpkin family? She might have thought twice about becoming his wife.

Corned beef and pastrami are made from **brisket,** a tasty but chewy cut of beef that needs a lot of cooking, as the word's origin suggests — it's probably from Old Norse *brjósk,* meaning "cartilage" or "gristle." Beef that is **corned** has been preserved in salt water. (*To corn* means "to reduce to grains," "to granulate.") Pastrami is beef that has been seasoned and smoked.

If brisket's too gristly (or grisly, if you don't believe in eating animals), go veggie and order Tofurky, a twentieth-century portmanteau brand name formed from *tofu* and *turkey.* On some menus, non-meat choices are indicated by alternative spellings like *chikken* or by scare quotes, a visual reminder to question a word: *"clam" chowder* is clam-less, made from crushed cashews. *"Crab" cakes* are crab-less, made from toasted pasta. Mr. Krabs (from the *SpongeBob SquarePants* TV series) would presumably approve.

Another popular choice for lunch is a salad, such as the **Cobb salad,** named after Robert Howard Cobb, owner of the Hollywood Brown Derby restaurant in Los Angeles. *Cobb salad* appears in print for the first time in 1947, but that's where certainty ends. Was it originally made in 1929, when the restaurant opened? Or in the middle of the night in 1937 or 1938, when Cobb was hungry and threw it together? Was one of his chefs responsible for this meal in a bowl that includes bacon, chicken, hard-boiled eggs, avocado, blue cheese, often three kinds of greens, and more? Some say it's the salad for those who don't really want salad.

The eponymously named **Caesar salad** has nothing to do with Julius Caesar; it's named for Caesar Cardini, a restaurateur who first made it in 1924 at the Hotel Caesar in Tijuana, Mexico. Cardini lived in San Diego but ran the hotel in Mexico to avoid U.S. Prohibition laws. A Caesar salad typically includes romaine lettuce, garlic, croutons, and anchovies and is dressed with raw or coddled egg, olive oil, lemon juice, and Parmesan cheese, though the egg is often omitted nowadays for fear of salmonella. (For more on *salad,* see p. 147.)

Still hungry after lunch and also on the run? Grab an eponymous candy bar, the **Baby Ruth.** Was the Baby Ruth named for the daughter of President Grover Cleveland, as the candy-bar makers once claimed, or for Babe Ruth, the baseball player? Lexicographers have put their money on Babe, saying the story about some other Ruth was a lawsuit dodge.

Maybe what you want for dessert — but righteously resist — is an ***Alice B. Toklas brownie,*** which would now be called a ***pot brownie.*** The popularity, or notoriety, of Alice B. Toklas brownies in the twentieth century might have been helped along by the 1968 Peter Sellers movie *I Love You, Alice B. Toklas.* In the film we see Toklas, a writer and the companion of Gertrude Stein, publishing a book containing a recipe for "Hashisch [*sic*] Fudge." Toklas did publish a cookbook in 1954, and it was a bestseller, but the hashish recipe came from a friend. Toklas (no connection with the word *toke,* which is of unknown origin) might never have made or eaten the product, but her name was attached to hashish brownies for decades.

Hashish derives from Arabic *hašīš,* "a dry herb from hemp leaves." Centuries ago, *hašīš* became associated with *assassin,* which derives from Latin *assassinus.* This Latin word was said to derive from Arabic *haššāš,* "hashish-eater," but this derivation has been challenged. More likely, *assassin* comes from *hašīšī,* a derogatory name in the Middle Ages for "a member of the Nizari sect of the Ismaili branch of Islam." Either way, hashish is part of the etymology of a name for a particular sect. The idea that they murdered enemies (both Christian and Muslim) under the influence of hashish spread via sensational tales, including Marco Polo's, probably with little basis in fact.

And while we're on the subject of ingested or inhaled drugs, a word or two about nicotine. This main active constituent of tobacco is a toxic alkaloid and was also used in insecticides. *Nicotine* is named after Jean Nicot, a sixteenth-century Frenchman who first brought the tobacco plant to France. He told the king it was medicinal; the king and a great many people agreed; and the rest is history we're still recovering from.

Other Eponyms Related to Lunch

Though it's not a food term, the *Heimlich maneuver* is intimately connected with eating, and it's an eponym. It comes from Dr.

Henry Heimlich, who invented the maneuver to dislodge food stuck in the trachea. Even though *Heimlich* often appears with the word *maneuver,* it can stand alone, and now it also has a life as a verb ("I had to *Heimlich* a guy in the restaurant"); maybe the moral is "Don't bite off more than you can chew."

And what about Doyley's doily? It, too, is physically connected with food, though not ingested. At first called a *napkin doily, doily* is now a stand-alone eponym, attributed to a seventeenth-century Mr. Doyley, who invented the lacy thing your pastry sits upon.

Off the Menu: Cicero's Nose

What's in a name? Sometimes food. One famous person with a food name is Marcus Tullius Cicero, the Roman orator, writer, and statesman (died 43 BCE). The *cicer* part of his name means "chickpea" in Latin, and perhaps the great orator's nose did look like a chickpea, as some have claimed. Google images of his bust — is there a little chickpea-like indentation at the end of his nose? Could be. More likely, however, the *cicer* in his name refers to his ancestors' agricultural business.

The name *Cicero* gave us the word *cicerone*, a "well-informed tour guide" who is eloquent, like Cicero. *Cicerone* also now means a "certified guide to beer drinking, a beer sommelier." Imagine any of the Founding Fathers or today's politicians or prizewinning writers becoming — in a few millennia — synonyms for "beer guide."

Toponyms

Many food terms are toponyms, meaning they derive from place-names (from Greek *topos,* "place," and *onoma,* "name"). We eat them for lunch.

Vichyssoise comes from Vichy, France, *Tabasco* from the Mexican city of Tabasco, and *jalapeños* from the Mexican city of Jalapa.

Bialy, a kind of flat bread with onions, derives from the city of Białystok, Poland. *Mayonnaise* comes from Mahón, Minorca, and *sardines* from Sardinia. The word *pheasant* derives from the city of Phasis, Georgia, in the Caucasus, where the bird may have originated.

In sixteenth-century English, the word *turkey* was originally applied to guinea fowl, which were imported through Turkey.

Subsequently, people in the New World used that word for the American bird.

Cotija, Gruyère, Edam, cheddar, Parmesan, and many other cheeses are named after their places of origin. Whether the Gruyère in your fridge is from the town of Gruyère, Switzerland, is another matter, having to do with legalities and who can own a name. Your Swiss cheese may be American.

The connection between food and place is almost now lost with *hamburger, frankfurter,* and *wiener,* which derive from Hamburg, Frankfurt, and Vienna, respectively. (*Hamburger, Frankfurter,* and *Wiener* are also demonyms, names referring to the inhabitants of a particular place. From Greek *dēmos,* "people," and *onoma,* "name.")

Various Americans claimed to have invented hamburgers, including the brothers Frank and Charles Menches, who said they served hamburgers in 1885 at the Erie County Fair in Hamburg, New York. Whether or not they were the first to serve a beef patty on a bun, the burger had gone all-American within a century. Partly because of U.S. fast-food chains, the burger went global as well. Shortened from hamburger, *burger* became a new combining form, as in *salmon burger, veggie burger,* and *nothing burger* (an insignificant thing, something lacking in substance).

The most outrageous of the many high-calorie burgers is probably the ***Luther burger,*** a hamburger with glazed doughnuts for

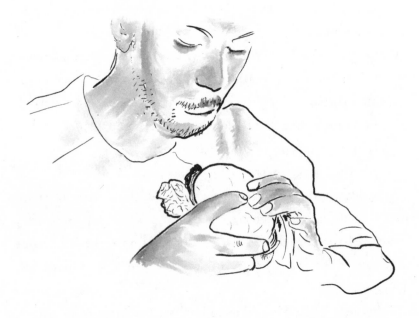

a bun. It's named after the twentieth-century singer and record producer Luther Vandross, who apparently loved — *really* loved — both doughnuts and burgers.

Hot dog for some people has replaced the words *frankfurter* and *wiener*. Its word history is even murkier than *hamburger*'s. *Hot dog* may be an example of a slang expression used by a particular group (in this case, perhaps college students who pushed the notion that the meat was canine) that then spread to the general population.

Want that dog or burger with fries and ketchup? ***French fries*** come not from France but from Belgium. It's the shape of the fries that is reflected in the word — as an adjective, *french* can mean "sliced lengthwise in strips." *Ketchup* comes from Chinese *ke-chiap*, "briny fish sauce," via Malay *kecap*, "soy sauce."

Bisque sounds like a toponym because of its association with the Bay of Biscay, where the lobster soup is served. But the word more likely derives from **biscuit**, ultimately from the Latin for "twice baked [bread]." Perhaps the soup is named for the bread served with it. A *biscuit-shooter*, by the way, is a person who serves food quickly, like a mess cook or speedy waiter.

Port, or *port wine*, comes from Oporto, Portugal, a major port from which the sweet dessert wine was shipped in the seventeenth century.

Sherry, white wine from Jerez (formerly called Xeres) de la Frontera in Andalusia is both a toponym and a back-formation. It derives from *Sherris* (or *Sherries*, a form of *Xeres*). *Sherris* is singular, but English speakers mistook it for a plural and lopped off the final *s*. The resulting word *sherry* sounded singular. (On back-formations, see pp. 15, 138, 188, 189–90.)

The **lima bean** takes its name from the city of Lima, Peru. The city in turn takes its name from the area, a valley called Limaq by early inhabitants who spoke Quechua. This South American language family, primarily spoken in the Peruvian Andes, has given English the words *jerky* and *quinoa*.

Marathon, Greece, has given us the word for a long race, based on the tradition that in 493 BCE, a messenger ran from Marathon to Athens (about twenty-five miles) to announce the Greeks' victory over the Persians. Besides being a toponym, *marathon* is part of an interesting, interconnected web of words. It means "fennel" in ancient Greek and came into Old English via Latin *faenum*, meaning "hay." *Fennel* and the Latin *faenum* are cognates with *female, fecund, felicity,* and *effete* (the last word meaning "worn out from bearing young").

U.S. CITIES WITH FOOD-BASED NAMES DERIVED FROM FIRST NATIONS LANGUAGES

Mahnomen (Minnesota) derives from Ojibwe, "wild rice."

Perkiomen (Pennsylvania) comes from Lenape and means "where there are cranberries."

Wysox (Pennsylvania), also from the Lenape language, means "place of grapes."

Chicago (Illinois) comes from the Miami-Illinois word for "wild leek."

Topeka (Kansas) perhaps derives from a Dakota word meaning "place for digging potatoes."

Food Words from Body Parts

Cabbage comes from Anglo-Norman *kaboche* (and variant forms from northern French), meaning "head," akin to Latin *caput,* also meaning "head." Before the word *cabbage* entered the English language, words like *colewort* and *kale* were used. Why the new word? Short answer: After the Norman Conquest, ambitious English speakers larded their English with French to sound classy. This borrowing of French resulted in many doublets pertaining to food:

cow and *beef, calf* and *veal, deer* and *venison, pig* and *pork, sheep* and *mutton*. One is food on your plate (*beef, veal, venison, pork, mutton*), the other an animal outside.

Cabbage may seem a plain food that wouldn't have acquired a classy name, but medieval cookbooks include cabbage prepared with saffron and bone marrow in elaborate meals for the rich. Greek and Roman writers extolled its virtues (saying it contributed to long life and good health) and occasionally noted its drawbacks (smelly if overcooked, postprandial flatulence). *Cabbage* can be a slur, as in *cabbagehead,* or a term of endearment, as in *my little cabbage.*

One's head is also a *bean*, a *nut* (from Old English *bēan* and *hnutu*), and the *upper crust.* Literally the top of a loaf, *upper crust* suggests high class in a slightly derogatory sense. It also meant "head" in the nineteenth century, as in a "handsome upper crust."

A nut-brain connection: the almond-shaped *amygdala,* gray matter in each cerebral hemisphere that's involved with emotions, comes from Greek *amugdalē,* meaning "almond."

The *lens* of the eye resembles the shape of a **lentil,** the literal meaning of *lens* in Latin. If you're eating lentils, you're eating eye lenses. And another eye-food connection: What people today call the "whites of the eyes," Shakespeare and others called the "*eggs* of the eyes."

Slang has given us *piehole* for mouth. Inside your piehole, you may have a *sweet tooth*. Kids have *milk teeth* that fall out as the permanent teeth come in.

Also in the piehole: a **tongue** (from Old English *tunge*), the human body part involved in eating and speaking; a word meaning "language" as well as "muscular organ in the mouth, important in taking in and swallowing food." The many cognates of the word *tongue* include language-related words like *lingo, bilingual,* and *linguist,* and food words like *linguine.*

Moving on down the bod, there are other terms that are both foods and body parts:

A **ladyfinger** is a small sponge cake. **Lady's-finger** is another term for **okra,** from the West African language Igbo *ọ̀kụ̀rụ̀,* a five-sided pod that might resemble a fist. *Okra* is also called *gumbo* (from Angolan *kingombo*).

A **knuckle,** from Dutch *knökel,* diminutive of *knoke,* "bone," is both a cut of meat, as in a knuckle of pork, and a joint of the finger. A **joint** is also, informally, an establishment for eating; for example, a burger joint. Or it can refer to a marijuana cigarette.

Cutlet comes from French *costelette,* "little rib," from Latin *costa,* "rib." In U.S. slang from the 1930s, *to rib* meant "to dupe or fool" someone, then "to tease."

Patella, "kneecap or kneepan," comes from Latin *patina,* "pan or shallow dish," which also gives us (via Spanish and Catalan) *paella* (see p. 169).

Ginseng derives from Chinese *rénshēn, rén,* "man," and *shēn,* "herb." The forked root of this plant resembles human legs, as does the forked root of the *mandrake,* from English *man* and *drake,* "dragon." Mandrake is poisonous but has been used in traditional medicine and in magic. According to folklore (and Harry Potter), the "man-dragon" shrieks when pulled from the earth. Ginseng also has been used medicinally and is found in some herbal teas and other drinks.

Womb is a body part we no longer find appetizing as a food word, but it used to be a delicacy. *Womb* in that case referred to the stomach (of a pig, sheep, or other animal) stuffed with *offal* (Old English *off* and *fall,* "remnants, cutoff parts"). *Womb* had a broad range of meanings, including "belly," "bowel," and "uterus," until well into early modern times, when the primary meaning became "uterus" and *womb* was no longer a term for human food. In the seventeenth century, the *placenta* (Latin for "flat cake") was called a *womb-cake.* Children are still, if rarely, called the *fruit of the womb.*

Here's a small, deviant Bad Lib alimentary billet-doux ("sweet note," "love letter"). Fill in the blanks using *stud muffin, sweetie pie, honey, hot buns, melons, snack, knead the dough, doubled in bulk, creamy, melted, lick it up,* and *pop it in the oven,* or change it all and use your own sexy, silly food words.

Oh, my darling, yummy _____[noun], when I see you naked with that spatula, I want to rub _____ [noun] all over your _____ [noun]. Let's _____ [verb] right now, and when it's _____ [adjective], we'll _____ [verb].

Food-Related Words for People

Humans can be *lampooners, lechers,* and *lickspittles,* all of which are connected, if indirectly, with drinking, via licking and lapping. *Lampoon,* "to satirize," comes from French *lampons,* "let's drink," from *lamper,* "to gulp down," from *laper,* "to lap up." A kin word of *lampoon* is *lambent,* "glowing or flickering," from Latin *lambere,* "to lick." *Lecher* comes from French, ultimately Old German, "to lick." A *lickspittle* (from Old English *liccian,* "to lick," and *spittan,* of imitative origin) is a toady or a sycophant, which brings us back to food — specifically figs.

A *sycophant* is an obsequious person like a lickspittle, but literally the word means "fig-showing" in Greek. As noted in the introduction, a *sycophant* was an informer, slanderer, or extorter in ancient Greece, and apparently his slander included "showing the fig" to the person he wanted to insult. It's a gesture that involves thrusting the thumb between two of the closed fingers of a fist. "Showing the fig" probably meant what "giving the finger" means today.

The word **shrimp** came into English in the fourteenth century, probably from the German *schrimpen,* "to shrivel up, to wrinkle." The English word meant both a puny person and a tasty crustacean. It's not certain which meaning came first, but it was probably the crustacean, and the name was then applied metaphorically to people. Thus a little creature spawned a human. (*Spawn* is from a Latin word meaning "to expand.")

Pasta names have come from body parts and other surprising sources. Match the different shapes of pasta (from Italian for "paste") with literal meanings.

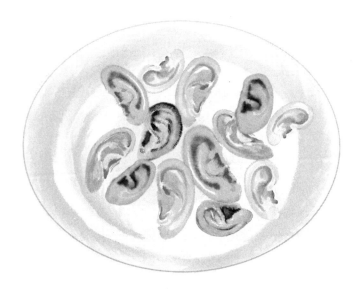

1. *capellini*
2. *conchiglie*
3. *campanelle*
4. *farfalle*
5. *fettuccine*
6. *manicotti*
7. *orecchiette*
8. *penne*
9. *spaghetti*
10. *strozzapreti*
11. *vermicelli*
12. *ziti*

(a) sleeves or muffs
(b) little worms
(c) little ears
(d) little strings
(e) little bells
(f) quill pens
(g) fine hair
(h) priest-stranglers
(i) newlyweds
(j) conch shells
(k) butterflies (and also bow ties)
(l) little ribbons

Answers: 1 (g), 2 (j), 3 (e), 4 (k), 5 (l), 6 (a), 7 (c), 8 (f), 9 (d), 10 (h), 11 (b), 12 (i)

Two or more correct answers: *molto bene*

More than two: *Astonishing;* one is *thunderstruck* (*astonish* and *thunderstruck* are both from Latin *ex,* "out," and *tonāre,* "to thunder").

In case you're wondering about the connection between ziti and newlyweds, *ziti* comes from *maccheroni di zita,* "macaroni of the bride," a wedding pasta. At some point *zita* (plural *zite*) changed to *ziti,* a masculine plural word. Insofar as any early meaning is preserved in the word, *ziti* arguably suggests both bride and groom, or perhaps gender fluidity, or simply newlyweds.

4

Happy Hour

Word Origins of Alcohol, Cocktails,
and Liquor Vessels

For many people, happy hour means time to unwind and hang out with friends after work, often at a bar and usually over a drink. For some, this means an alcoholic drink.

Alcohol derives from Arabic *al-kuhl,* "the kohl." In the sixteenth century, the term referred to powders, especially a black powder called *kohl* (antimony sulfide or lead sulfide) that was used as eye makeup. It also meant "spirit" or "liquid essence" obtained by distillation, a process of heating and cooling that yields a concentrated liquid. By the eighteenth century, *spirits* in English referred to distilled fermented liquids such as whiskey, brandy, gin, and rum, and *alcohol* meant the intoxicating ingredient in any drinkable liquid.

Most likely the earliest alcoholic drink that humans consumed was fermented honey mixed with water; humans in many places around the world were making fermented honey drinks as early as 10,000 BCE and possibly earlier. A fermented honey drink required no cultivating of the soil, no cooking, and no preparation other than mixing it with water. But making this drink did involve risk and skill in getting honey from the bees. According to some myths, it also required chastity on the part of the honey-gatherer to maintain the purity of the honey. The rewards for the successful honey-gatherer were great: sweet food, sweet drink, and *intoxication*. (Delightful to experience, but the etymology may be sobering—it's from Latin *intoxicāre*, from *in-*, "into," and *toxicāre*, "to poison.")

We call a fermented honey drink **mead,** from Old English *me(o)du*, "mead," deriving from the Indo-European root *medhu*, "honey." This root also gave us the word *amethyst*, an interesting word in light of alcohol. It's from Greek *amethustos* (from *a-*, prefix meaning "not," and *methustos*, "be drunk"). In classical times, drinking goblets were sometimes adorned with amethysts because the "not-be-drunk" stone was thought to prevent drunkenness. *Amethyst* was also the name of a purple vine that was similar in color to the precious stone but with "good-for-nothing" grapes that yielded an almost nonalcoholic wine, as Pliny the Elder reports in his *Natural History* (77 CE).

The word *mead* has been in the English language for more than a thousand years and has changed relatively little in form or meaning, like *ale, beer,* and *wine. Ale* derives from Old English *alu, ealu; beer* is from Old English *bēor,* in turn from Latin *bibere,* "to drink"; and *wine* is from Old English *wīn,* influenced by Latin *vīnum.*

Here are a few notable words pertaining to beer, ale, and wine that a **gourmet** (originally, "wine taster") will want to use. *Noble rot* sounds unappealing, but it's a good thing—a mold intentionally cultivated on certain grapes to help produce a sweet wine. Drinks that are *mulled* (of unknown origin) or *muddled* (from a Middle English word meaning "to wallow in mud") have been mixed with sugar and spices.

Bragget (or *bragot*) is ale mulled with fermented honey. It's an old drink that's becoming popular again, although now it's mulled with sugar instead of honey, frequently spiced with cinnamon, and often served warm.

Off the Menu: The Grapevine

Rumors spreading through the grapevine may include *vignettes,* or short, evocative accounts of someone or something. *Vignette* and its related form *vinet* (sometimes spelled *vignet*) come from the Latin *vīnum,* "wine." The earliest meaning of *vinet* was an ornamental border of a medieval manuscript. These borders were often illustrations of trailing vines, with leaves, tendrils, and embellishments that might include drawings of animals and humans, sometimes engaged in unusual behaviors (animals dressed in clothing and hunting humans; nuns playing ball; bare bums mooning us from amid the grape leaves) that seem at odds with the religious text framed by the vines.

The word *vignette* also refers to any small design on a page in a book, often at the beginning or end of a chapter. It's like a *dingbat* (of uncertain etymology), an ornamental character or glyph used by printers. A *dingbat* also has the fruit of the vine in its past, having formerly meant "any strong drink."

Some exercise trainers call a workout session a happy hour because of the endorphin-induced bliss you may receive by flexing your *muscles* (from Latin *musculus*, "little mouse") and firing your *glutes* (the *gluteus maximus*, biggest of three muscles in the backside, from Greek *gloutos*, "buttock"). *Happy hour* in this workout sense reflects the earliest meaning of the expression, which comes from turn-of-the-twentieth-century U.S. Navy jargon and meant "time set aside for entertainment, especially boxing and wrestling."

Soon after, movies and vaudeville acts, and sometimes female dancers hired from clubs, contributed to the hour's (or hours') happiness. Alcohol was at various times forbidden by navy rules and of course illegal during Prohibition, but eventually alcohol became part of on-board happy hours. By the 1950s, the expression *happy hour* had jumped ship. Onshore, it came to mean reduced-price cocktails and other drinks at a bar or restaurant served in the late afternoon.

The word ***cocktail*** includes roosters and horses in its past. It first referred to a horse's tail that was docked (or cut), which made it stick up in a manner resembling a cock's perky tail. But what does a horse's tail, cocked, docked, or hanging freely, have to do with a mixed drink?

It's a question of purity. The tails of carriage and hunting horses were often cut, but the tail of a thoroughbred racehorse would not have been. If a cocktailed horse was found to be part of a racehorse's lineage, its pedigree was mixed, impure, adulterated.

Hearing this, the happy-hour drinker responds, "Why impugn my Bloody Mary? It's a mixed drink, but that doesn't mean it's impure or adulterated."

Right. In the nineteenth century, when the meaning of *cocktail* became a "mixed drink," it was
used in a positive sense. It meant
alcohol (usually distilled spirits) mixed
with bitters, water, sugar, or liqueur.

There are many cocktails in a mixologist's
brain, and here are a few with a twist of whimsy,
or, as in the first example below, gallows humor.
These cocktail names often refer to the

place where the drink was invented and sometimes to a person, real or imagined. They are almost all from the twentieth century, and most of the names are coinages—words entering the language because someone or some group chose the name, probably for marketing purposes, and it stuck. (See coining in the introduction, p. 15.)

A **Bloody Mary,** vodka and seasoned tomato juice, is named after Mary Tudor, half sister of Elizabeth I and daughter of Henry VIII and his first wife, Catherine of Aragon. Mary reigned briefly, from 1553 to 1558, and during this short time, as part of an attempt to undo her father's religious reformation, she had more than 280 dissenters killed. Hence the nickname "Bloody Mary," in use by at least 1652. The earliest recorded date of *Bloody Mary* as a name for a cocktail isn't until 1939, when it was noted in the *New York Herald Tribune* as a new "pick-me-up."

The Bloody Mary cocktail gave birth to the **Virgin Mary** mocktail, which is a Bloody Mary without the vodka. Other mocktails include the **Shirley Temple,** made with ginger ale, grenadine, and a maraschino cherry and named after the child actress, and the **Roy Rogers,** made with cola, grenadine, and a maraschino cherry and named after a singing cowboy actor. **Mocktail** is an early-twentieth-century word, a blending of *mock* and *tail.* It's faux, it's fun, it fits into happy hour. There are many delicious mocktails, and they're always an excellent choice.

One more fact about Bloody Mary Tudor: She should not be confused with Mary, Queen of Scots, who lost her head (also a bloody affair) when Queen Elizabeth I was on the throne. And two facts, one well known and one trivial, about Elizabeth I's long and noteworthy reign, from 1558 to 1603: She was called the Virgin Queen (after whom the state of Virginia is named), and she has no eponymous *cocktail* or *mocktail*.

Off the Menu: #%$&

To some ears, the word *bloody* is swearing. It's now considered only mild swearing, but it may still be offensive to some or inappropriate in polite company. One explanation for the use of *bloody* as swearing says that it's a euphemistic alteration of "by Our Lady," but lexicographers tend to reject this claim for lack of textual references. So, too, with the explanation that *bloody* as swearing derives from a blasphemous reference to the blood of Christ; the earliest instances of the term as an adjectival intensifier don't bear out this claim. Nevertheless, even if the word didn't begin as sacrilegious, it took on the force of blasphemy. Those who were offended at the word didn't care what lexicographers thought.

It's likely that *bloody* comes from a slang term for aristocrats, *bloods*. The term then came to mean not only the aristocrats but their supposed drunken ways. A *bloody drunk* was "drunk as a blood" or "drunk as a lord."

A suave and sophisticated citizen of the world in need of a cocktail would order a ***cosmopolitan*** (usually vodka, Cointreau, cranberry juice, and lime juice). The name comes from Greek *kosmopolitēs*, from *kosmos*, "world," and *politēs*, "citizen."

Sex on the Beach first happened in Fort Lauderdale in the 1960s. Not quite on the beach but in a bar called Confetti, and it was such a big hit that many people thereafter decided to give Sex on the Beach a try—that is, order a cocktail containing vodka, peach schnapps, orange juice, and cranberry juice (or some prefer grenadine). A rose by any other name may or may not smell as sweet, but a cocktail named Sex on the Beach will sell better than "new vodka drink" during spring break in Fort Lauderdale.

The ***Manhattan,*** made of whiskey and vermouth and some-times a dash of bitters, takes its name from a place and from the people who live there, so the Manhattan cocktail is both a top-onym and an eponym. *Manhattan,* or *Manathans,* may mean "gathers bows" or "where one gathers bows." Dutch settlers bought or took the island in 1626 from the indigenous people whom the Dutch called Manathans. The name was borrowed into English as *Manhattan*. (For more on place-names from First Nations, see p. 107, and *tuxedo*, p. 194.)

Whiskey, part of a Manhattan cocktail, came into English from Scottish Gaelic *uisge beatha or* Irish Gaelic *uisce beathadh*, meaning "water of life." The earliest English forms of the word, *uskebeaghe, usquebaugh*, etc., appeared in the sixteenth century; *whiskey* (or *whisky, whiskie*) appeared in the early eighteenth century. **Vermouth,** also in a Manhattan, is from German *wermuth*, "wormwood," a mildly toxic plant with a bitter flavor and a long history as a medicine (for stomach trouble, for example). It's also used as a pesticide against moths, fleas, and worms.

Wormwood is also used in ***absinthe*** (a potent, usually green alcoholic spirit, from Greek *apsinthion*, "wormwood"). Because of the supposed crazy-making properties of wormwood, absinthe was banned in the United States from 1912 until 2007, but it is now generally considered no more crazy-making than other alcoholic drinks.

Drinking absinthe often involves an amusing ritual and a special spoon: Put a sugar cube or two on top of a slotted spoon, rest the spoon over a glass of absinthe, and pour ice water over the cubes (or light them on fire). Then watch as sugar melts through the slots into the drink and makes the clear liquid milky. The process is called *louching*, possibly from *louche*, meaning "a disreputable, rakish person," from Old French *losche,* "squint-eyed," from Latin *luscus,* "blind in one eye."

The name **mai tai** probably derives from Tahitian *maita'i,* meaning "good, pleasant." The main claimant to the title of mai tai inventor is Victor J. Bergeron, owner of Trader Vic's restaurant in Oakland, California. First concocted in the 1940s or 1950s, this cocktail is made with rum, curaçao, and fruit juice. The mai tai became the iconic drink of faux-tiki culture, a Hollywood-inspired, romanticized view of Polynesian culture especially evident in bars that were decorated with fake tiki sculptures and served drinks with names like **Singapore sling.** (This drink, consisting of **gin,** ultimately from Latin *jūniperus,* "juniper" [berry], and cherry brandy or another liqueur, was developed long before Hollywood-y tiki culture, probably about 1915, by bartender Ngiam Tong Boon in Singapore.) Tiki culture in the United States faded toward the end of the twentieth century, but the mai tai remains a popular drink.

A **Harvey Wallbanger** is made from vodka, orange juice, and Galliano (a vanilla-and-anise-flavored liqueur). The LA bartender Donato "Duke" Antone claimed he created this cocktail, but the name was probably coined by some staffer in a marketing department associated with Galliano (and someone named Harvey?).

The **sidecar** traditionally consists of cognac, orange liqueur, and lemon juice shaken with ice, strained into a glass, and served with a sugared rim. It was probably invented in the early 1920s, possibly by a U.S. Army captain who was stationed in France and often rode in a friend's sidecar to Harry's New York Bar in Paris. Maybe the captain was grateful for a ride (even if it was in the small, one-wheeled vehicle attached to a motorcycle) and wanted to honor his friend by dubbing the new drink a *sidecar*. Or perhaps the captain didn't like being on the side of the motorcycle, white-knuckling it as the friend drove him around bends, the small car airborne on the curve, then landing with a thud. Maybe he always arrived with a headache and needed that cocktail as a sidecar cure.

The **martini** was first called a *Martinez,* referring to the town of Martinez, California; the drink—gin (or vodka) and vermouth with an olive or a twist of lemon—was supposedly concocted for gold-rushers. But the cocktail is also connected to a partner in an Italian firm selling vermouth—Martini and Rossi. *Martini* replaced *Martinez* as the more common name for the drink.

Martini has given us a productive suffix, *-tini.* It shows up in many cocktail names, like Flirtini, from the series *Sex and the City.*

If you were to invent your own mixed drink, what would you call it? *Bookatini,* if you like to chill with a cocktail and a novel. *Schlepitini,* if you've had a long commute. Or if you just got fired, you might call your drink a *Fuckitini* (or a *F**kitini,* if you like the coy asterisks). Scribble the ingredients and the name of your *-tini* in the margin of this book.

Many cocktail names lack the *-tini*. For example, the ***piña colada*** (Spanish for "strained pineapple") is a rum, coconut cream, and pineapple juice cocktail blended with ice and garnished with a pineapple wedge or maraschino cherry. Some claim the drink started in Cuba, but Ramón Marrero usually gets the credit for inventing the cocktail at the Caribe Hilton, San Juan, Puerto Rico, in 1954. Some prefer a pirate story in which Roberto Cofresí, a nineteenth-century marauder at sea, invented the rum drink to boost his crew's morale. (Why the low morale? Nagging consciences because of the pirating, perhaps?) The story sounds apocryphal, but piña colada lovers would likely agree that the drink lifts one's spirits.

The cocktail called ***fuzzy navel*** contains peach schnapps and orange juice, sometimes with a splash of vodka. The drink was created in the 1980s by the National Distillers marketers and an ad agency; *fuzzy* refers to the peach and *navel* to the orange.

A ***terremoto,*** from the Spanish word for "earthquake," is a cocktail named after the 1985 earthquake in Chile. It's made with white wine, pineapple ice cream, and grenadine. If you order a second one of these cocktails, it's an *aftershock.*

The cocktail called ***vesper*** (or *vesper martini*) originally consisted of gin, vodka, and Kina Lillet (an aperitif wine from Bordeaux containing quinine; it's no longer available). The word *vesper* can refer to the evening star named after the god Hesperus, but the same star is also—perhaps confusingly—called Venus. *Vespers* (in the plural) refers to a service of evening prayers in Western Christian churches.

But the cocktail called vesper derives not from the star or the prayers, but from a novelist. Ian Fleming created the drink in the 1953 novel *Casino Royale,* which was popularized by the James Bond film. In novel and film, the cocktail is nameless until Bond meets the beautiful Vesper Lynd, after whom he decides to name the cocktail. *Vesper,* however, has often been misheard by film audiences as *vespa.* To an American ear, *vesper* may indeed sound like *vespa,* which is the name of a motorbike and also means "wasp" in Italian.

What's in a name? A god and goddess, bright star, heavenly body, prayer and worship, zippy motorbike, and stinging wasp. The cocktail called vesper packs a wallop—except **wallop** in British English can mean beer, which is one thing a vesper does not contain. Some bartenders think the vesper is not something a mixologist would invent. ("Gin *and* vodka?" is a typical bartender's response, said with a sneery lip.)

A stirred cocktail might ruffle Bond's feathers, but for others, stirring a liquid can be a rousing experience. In the world of beer-making, to *rouse* means "to stir," and it's best done with a brewer's paddle. In the world of falconry, to *rouse* refers to a bird ruffling its feathers.

A Cinematic-Lexicographical Pub Quiz

In the cinematic world of Bond, *to rouse* means:

    A. To give your Vespa a lube job

    B. To excite a wasp

    C. To ruffle your opponents in a poker game by wearing a tight dress

    D. All of the above

Answer: A, B, C, and D. In the spirit of happy hour, everyone's a winner.

For being a good sport, treat yourself to some *tapas,* the bite-size foods often eaten in bars. Like appetizers, tapas include a wide range of foods — marinated olives, caviar on crackers, fried squid, chorizo-filled dates, toast with creamy white beans, meatballs, perhaps a *chimichanga* (from Mexican Spanish for "trinket"), vegan choices like dates stuffed with cashew "goat cheese," and more. *Tapas* comes from Spanish *tapa,* "cover, lid," because *tapas* were served on small plates or saucers placed on the tops of drinks, like lids.

Off the Menu: On the Sofa

A **canapé** is a small piece of bread or pastry with a tasty topping. It's a little more substantial than an amuse-bouche (p. 195), and it's more or less the same as a tapa or appetizer, except appetizers are followed by a meal. Canapés are often served at receptions or parties, the sort of food you eat with your fingers while you're standing. If you're tired of standing and a comfy sofa happens to be close by, how lucky and appropriate, because *canapé* in French means "couch" or "sofa" — a suitable

receptacle for your hams, so *ploppez-vous* (faux French for "take a load off"). *Canapé* is related to *canopy*, which long ago meant a "couch with mosquito curtains" and ultimately comes from Greek *kōnōps*, "mosquito." To many a mosquito, we are the tasty topping on a sofa.

Glasses and Other Vessels for Drinks

Containers, such as oaken barrels, may affect flavor. Habits and expectations about the shape and look of what one drinks from can affect enjoyment as well as one's perception of taste—some people refuse to drink champagne out of a wineglass, insisting on a classic coupe (usually a stemmed glass with a wide shallow cup, from Latin *cuppa*, "cup," via French *coupe*, "cup, goblet"). Vessels for alcohol have been wooden, leather, pewter, glass, ceramic, aluminum, plastic—any material that's reasonably watertight.

Glass descends from the Indo-European root *ghel-*, "to shine." This root generated a big family of words in Germanic languages, Sanskrit, Greek, Latin, Polish, Syriac, and Old Iranian. Some English cognates of *glass* include *yellow, glisten, gold,* and *zloty* (Polish money, meaning "golden") but also *gall, cholera, melancholy* (from Greek *kholē,* "bile"), and *felon* (from dialectal Latin *fel,* "bile"). Shininess and luster have been valued for ages, it would seem, but not dull yellow — as is evident in the words derived from bile, the greenish-yellow digestive juice made in the liver.

Glass in modern English has a great many meanings, including as a noun, "vessel to hold liquid," and as a verb, "to lift a glass to," as when you make a *toast. Toast* in this sense comes from the centuries-old practice of putting a piece of spiced toast in a glass of wine and drinking to the health of a lady. The word *toast* was figuratively applied to the woman; there are many eighteenth-century examples of *toast* meaning a woman who has the honor of being *toasted.* We no longer refer to a person as a toast, except in the expressions *toast of the town* ("someone greatly admired") and, quite the opposite, *that person is toast,* meaning "in serious trouble." A *toast* is also an improvised rhythmic speech or narrative, akin to rap, recited over a recorded soundtrack.

Glasses for Wine and Cocktails

The large mouth on a cocktail glass with a round bowl allows your nose to enjoy the aroma to the max, and the V-shaped martini glass, with its steep-angled sides, may keep ingredients mixed. The

bigger bowl for the red-wine glass helps with swirling and aerating, and the stem on a wineglass prevents your hand from heating the wine too much. Even a red wine shouldn't be above 68 degrees F, and white wine not more than 55 degrees. But not all drinks are meant to stay cool; brandy, for instance, is served in a ***snifter,*** which has a short stem so that you can cradle the bowl and keep the brandy warmish. (For more on snifters, see "Nightcaps," p. 199.)

Champagne is often drunk from the tall, narrow glass called a ***flute*** (from Old French *flahute* or Provençal *flaut,* referring to a flutelike instrument). But some say the narrow opening of a flute limits the supply of oxygen reaching the champagne, which affects the flavor, and that a coupe, tulip, or wineglass would be better. (Rumor on the web says that 1950s or 1960s marketers wanted to make champagne more appealing to the male consumer, so they shaped the glass like a woman's breast, and that's how coupes came to exist. But evidence for this? None, it would seem.) Pro-flutists argue that too much surface area means the champagne will fizzle too fast and go flat. Everyone at least agrees a flute lets you enjoy the sight and feel of bubbles shooting up and bursting.

Champagne is also a toponym, coming from an area in northeastern France where the sparkling wine was first made in about 1700. The word *champagne* is sometimes written with a capital *C,* as it's a fiercely guarded proprietary name, but that applies only to sparkling wine from the Champagne region.

For Storing and Pouring Wine and Liquor

Bottle is related to ***butt,*** in the sense of a large wooden container; *bottle* and *butt* both derive ultimately from Latin *buttis,* "cask," and both bottles and butts store wine, beer, and ale. (*Butt* meaning "rear end" might be a back-formation from *buttocks.*)

Historically, a ***flagon*** was a large pewter, wooden, or ceramic container, usually with a handle and spout, used for serving drinks.

Now the term *flagon* also means a large glass bottle with a neck that holds about twice the amount a normal wine bottle holds (a normal bottle holds 750 milliliters, about 25 ounces).

A *flask* is any smallish, usually portable container for liquid — or gunpowder — made of wood, leather, horn, metal, or glass. *Flagon* and *flask* are etymologically related, both coming from Old French *flacon*, and the English word *fiasco* is also related to *flagon* and *flask*. It comes from the Italian *far fiasco*, "make a bottle," but how it came to mean "a complete disaster" or "big fat royal mess" is anyone's guess.

Like a flagon, a **magnum** (the neuter form of Latin *magnus*, "great") holds twice the amount of a normal wine bottle. A **jeroboam** is even bigger, holding about four times as much. The name of the big bottle comes from an ancient king of Israel, Jeroboam, who was "a mighty man of valor" (in 1 Kings 11:28).

For Storing, Pouring, and Drinking Beer

The wide mouth of the slightly tapering, cylindrical, pint-size beer glass lets you get your nose close to the surface as the beer releases aromas. Those aromas titillate. A *goblet*, from French *gobelet*, "little cup," has a wide bowl that also allows the nose to get right down there and smell the goods. The wide bowl accommodates foam and works well for heavy beers, including **bock.** Despite web rumors, a bock beer doesn't have anything to do with a goat. *Bock* refers to a place, the German town of Einbeck.

A **spritzer,** from German *spritzen,* "to squirt," consists of white wine (or prosecco) and carbonated water and is often served in a **highball glass,** though practices vary greatly. The story told about the highball glass originating in the dining car of a train is happy-hour fare (and unlikely): Drinks had to be served in tall glasses to prevent spilling when the steam engine got up to speed. At the train's top speed, indicated in the engine room by a ball showing the boiler pressure was high, the engine and the guests with drinks in tall glasses were *highballing.*

A **lowball glass** is stable, unlikely to tip, and good for drinking spirits *neat,* "not diluted or mixed with other ingredients" (from French *net,* "clean"). This glass is also called a **rocks glass,** for whiskey on ice.

Both highball and lowball glasses are **tumblers,** "drinking glasses with straight sides and flat bottoms." But old tumblers had rounded bottoms and wouldn't sit flat on the table. If you put the filled glass down, the liquid would spill, so it was bottoms up for drinkers (unless you chose to hold and nurse the drink rather than chug it. Not cool).

A common way (at least in parts of Europe and some American bars) to drink beer is from a glass mug with a handle. The word *mug* is of uncertain origin but is probably Scandinavian, akin to Swedish *mugg*, "pitcher of beer." One of the many meanings of *mug* as a verb is "to drink excessively," and as a noun, it means "a funny or ugly face," probably from eighteenth-century English mugs that were formed into exaggerated faces (also called Toby mugs). If the beer mug is made of ceramic, an American might call it a **beer stein** (literally "beer stone" in German). But if you don't want to sound like a tourist, don't order a stein of beer in a German-speaking area. *Ein bier, bitte* ("A beer, please") will do, and then be prepared to answer the question *Gross oder klein?* ("Large or small?").

In English, the term *beer stone* refers to the scaly stuff (calcium oxalate) that forms on the inside of vats. Calcium oxalate can also occur inside humans in the form of kidney stones.

A **tankard** is a beer mug with a handle, a hinged lid, and a thumb lever to operate the lid.

Supposedly the lid was invented to keep out flies and other pests. Perhaps it served that purpose but was a later addition to the tankard. In Middle English, *tankard* meant a "large open tub," and there's no indication that the tub had a lid or a bung (as for the hole of a cask) or other stopper.

A *jug,* however, has a tight-fitting cap around a narrow mouth. *Jug* comes from a nickname for Joan, Joanna, or Jenny. From woman to beer container—how did the transfer of meaning happen? Perhaps through an association of beer or ale with those who made and served it; historically, they were very often women.

Tapster comes from Old English *tæppestre,* "a woman who drew ale for sale." By the late fourteenth century, almost four hundred years after its first occurrence in writing, the term also referred to men. Another century later, *tapster* was used as a derogatory term for a woman, but apparently not for a man.

Brewster, from Old English *brēowan,* "brew," and -*ster,* a suffix indicating a feminine-agent noun, referred to women brewers. About the same time (1300), the word *brewer* came into use, referring to men. Some seventy years later, the formerly female *brewster* could refer to men as well as women, about the time that men began to take over the brewing business.

An *alewife* was "a woman who brews or sells ale or who owns a tavern." In medieval and early modern England, alewives were often represented as fat, deceptive, sexually provocative, and uncontrollable. Perhaps an aspect of this stereotype crossed the Atlantic and manifested itself, surprisingly, in the name of a fish. Seventeenth-century North American colonists referred to shad (or possibly herring) as *alewives,* supposedly because the belly of the fish resembled an alewife's paunch.

During the centuries when brewing went from women's work to a male-dominated industry, the words *tapster* and *alewife* took on derogatory meanings, a fate that the word *brewer* didn't suffer, though brewers and alewives were presumably equally honest or dishonest.

A **growler** is a jug by another name, bought and filled at a brewery and brought home. It holds about two quarts and is refillable. If you want half that amount, get a **crowler** (from "canned growler"), but it comes in a can that's not refillable. *Growlers* are very popular now, and they've been around for more than a century, though they used to be pails and buckets rather than corked or capped jugs. (Think of the song lyric "Frankie went down to the corner / just for a bucket o' beer.") The written references to *growlers* from the late nineteenth century often occur in the expression *rush the growler,* which means both "to fetch a bucket of beer from a saloon" and "to drink copiously." The origin of the word *growler* as beer container is unknown, though of course a story has made the rounds: that the beer in the bucket "growled" and hissed through a lid as one rushed home with it. More to the point, the word *rush* can mean "to make a big noise." *Rush the growler* suggests "roaring drunk." (For more, see "Nightcaps," p. 199.)

Off the Menu: Silly Hour

Silly used to mean "happy," "blissful," even "blessed." It was good to be silly. But over the centuries, the word became increasingly negative. At one stage in this semantic development, a *silly* person was "helpless," "feeble," and "ignorant." A century later, *silly* meant "foolish," "frivolous," "lacking judgment," and these possibly happy-hour-like qualities still inhere in the word *silly*.

But happy hour can potentially draw people together. Carousing with others, with or without alcohol, can make one feel happy, blissful, even blessed — *silly* in the old sense of the word.

Feeling *silly* in the "blessed" sense, let's go to dinner.

5

Dinner

Word Origins of Veggies, Meats, Nuts, and Sweets

There's a symmetry to the first and last meals of the day insofar as they both mean "to break one's fast." *Dinner* (and *dine*) ultimately go back to Latin *disjējūnāre* or *disiēiūnāre*, "to break one's fast." (For more, including the time of day one might eat dinner, see "Breakfast," p. 21.)

Let's say for dinner you want a salad and a steak, with your **dressing** (from Old French *dresser*, "arrange," "prepare") on the side, and your *salad* (from Latin *sal*, "salt") consists of raw *vegetables* (from Latin *vegēre*, "to grow").

Off the Menu: Sass

Sass, sassy, saucy, and soused all go back to Latin sal, meaning "salt." So do the words salsa, salad, salami, sausage, and salary. Roman soldiers were given money, called a salarium, to buy salt, and their salarium is the basis of our word salary. Salad means "having been salted." It derives, along with salsa, sauce, saucy, sausage, and salami, from Latin salsa (feminine form of *salsus*), meaning "salted." But *salsus/salsa* also meant "humorous," "sharp," and "witty," which helps explain the meaning of the English words *saucy*, *sassy* (a variant of *saucy*), and *sass* (back-formation from the earlier word *sassy*).

Sass meaning "back talk" came into English in the nineteenth century. But *sass*, like *sauce*, was also a word for vegetables and fruit, as in *long sass*, meaning carrots and parsnips, and *short sass*, meaning potatoes, onions, and turnips. *To souse* in Middle English meant "to soak in liquid," often salty liquid, thus "to brine or pickle food." Since the early seventeenth century, *soused* has also meant intoxicated. A *soused* brain may be *sassy* but probably not very sharp. *Salsa*, besides being a spicy sauce, is lively dance music, incorporating elements of jazz and rock and originating in Latin America.

Eating that salad followed by steak means going from raw to cooked food, and this progression provides an opportunity for us to consider in small ways (including etymology of course) the theory that eating cooked food ushered in *culture* (customs, arts, institutions, laws; from Latin *colere,* "to tend, cultivate").

Cooking food entailed controlling fire, organizing socially, and making vessels to cook in, among other accomplishments. Eating cooked food meant spending much less time chewing and digesting. (Chimps spend five hours a day chewing. Cows spend six or more hours a day.) *Ruminating* (Latin *rūmināre*, "to chew over") for humans means not chewing but thinking—about recipes we love to read but may never make, about the pleasure of watching baking shows, about the transformation that cooking promises, and, for the moment, about the meaning of *raw*.

From Old English *hrēaw*, *raw* is part of a family of words, including *crude* and *cruel*, that derive from the Indo-European root *kreuə-*, meaning "raw flesh." In some contexts, *raw* has negative implications, such as "uncivilized," "immature," and "unrefined." But *raw* has a range of meanings, including positive ones, such as "realistic," "frank," "honest." We love many raw foods, if not raw flesh, and believe they're good for us.

Here are some of the uncooked veggies we love in a salad. (For *lettuce*, from Latin *lact-*, "milk," see p. 94. And for a discussion of *romaine*, from French *laitue romaine*, "Roman lettuce," see the introduction, pp. 6–9.)

Arugula, also called ***rocket,*** comes from Italian (regional variant) *aruculu* or *rucol*, from Latin *ērūca*, "rocket" or "colewort," a cabbage-like plant. The word *arugula* derives from the

Indo-European root *ghers-*, "to bristle," and perhaps we sense a bit of that ancestry in the peppery taste of arugula.

The word **pepper,** from Old English *piper,* with roots going back to Sanskrit *pippalī,* "berry, peppercorn," refers to black peppercorns and the tongue- and nose-prickling powder made from them. But *pepper* also refers to the hollow, elongated or bell-shaped vegetables that we call hot peppers and sweet peppers. Botanically they're fruits, but in the kitchen, they're vegetables. The 1892–93 Supreme Court case *Nix v. Hedden* ruled that even though tomatoes (and peppers) were classified botanically as fruits, they were vegetables according to culinary usage, including whether the food was eaten as a main course or dessert. Thus, the Tariff Act of 1883, which imposed a tax on imported vegetables, remained in effect. Fruits were not taxed.

Words formed from *pepper* suggest its liveliness. *Pep, pep talk, pep rally,* all invoke the idea of high spirits. But *pepper spray,* made from cayenne pepper, which can cause acute distress to eyes and respiratory passages, shows the powerful effects of capsaicin, the compound that makes the mouth feel on fire.

A **carrot** seems as common and old as the hills and sounds as Old English-y as *pepper,* so perhaps it's surprising that the word *carrot* was not part of English until the late fifteenth century, coming via French and Latin, from Greek *karōton.* Again the question

arises: Could the food have been in the diet if the word for it wasn't in the language?

The answer: a qualified yes. Even if they didn't have the word *carrot*, English speakers could have been eating it or something like it for centuries. The carrot wasn't cultivated until 900 CE in central Asia, but a white-colored "wild carrot" was indigenous to England and was probably one of a number of foods referred to by *walhmore, wealmoru,* and other compounds from Old English *moru* ("edible root"). To complicate matters, the word **parsnip** (from Latin *pastinus,* "tool for planting seeds") was used for what we would call a carrot *and* what we would call a parsnip. They're both long, tapering edible roots with a fairly sweet flavor. *Parsnip* eventually (by the late fifteenth century) came to refer only to the white root and *carrot* to the orange root vegetable.

In modern taxonomy, carrot and parsnip, as well as parsley and celery, belong to the family Umbelliferae. It's not surprising that what people today consider different but related plants were sometimes called by the same name. Or that in the complicated process of one culture acquiring new foods from other cultures, names were garbled. Or that we simply can't be sure today what a word meant centuries ago.

Celery had a circuitous route into the English language, from Greek to Latin to Italian to French *céleri,* finally becoming *celery* in English in the seventeenth century. There was a wild form of celery called *smallage* in Middle English, but the word was eventually replaced by *celery*, which—brace yourself—comes from Greek *selinon*, meaning "parsley." **Parsley** comes from Old English *petersilie*, influenced by Old French *peresil* and ultimately from Greek *petroselinon* (*petro*, "rock," and "parsley"). But eventually (in the seventeenth century), the greenery got sorted out, at least from the modern point of view. *Celery* referred to the green stalks we're familiar with today, what botanists call *Apium graveolens*. And *parsley* referred to the leafy green herb that we're familiar with today and that botanists call *Petroselinum crispum*.

What's in a name? One crumb of truth at the bottom of this word salad is that language is always changing. Who knows what will happen to the word *celery* in five hundred years?

Off the Menu: What's Up, Doc?

A *carrot* is a veggie, bought by the bunch or bag. A *carat* is a unit of measure especially used for diamonds, which are not usually bought by the bunch or bag. Though *carat* has nothing to do with *carrot*, the etymology of *carat* includes food, being derived from the Greek for *carob bean*. And then there's the *karat*. It's a measure for the purity of gold, though sometimes it's simply a variant spelling of *carat*, used for both diamonds and gold. And what about *caret*? A *caret* is the editor's mark ^ (or ⌃ or ⅄) usually placed below a line to indicate where something needs to be inserted. In Latin, *caret* means "it is lacking," and the lacking word or phrase is usually written above the ^.

Here's one more example of an old word that served as an umbrella term for four vegetables before it finally narrowed in meaning. The Old English word *cipa* (from Latin *cēpa, caepa,* "onion") probably referred to the vegetables we now call *onions, shallots, scallions,* and *chives.* Later, in Middle English, *cipa* came to refer only to chives, and the words *onion, shallot,* and *scallion* were borrowed (with their modern meanings) into English.

Onion came via Anglo-Norman and French from Latin *ūnion,* meaning "a large pearl," from *ūnus,* "one." (Bit of a head-scratcher—but at least an onion sort of looks like a pearl.) **Shallot** came from French *eschalotte,* and **scallion** from the

Latin name for a seaport in the Mideast, *Ascalon*. So it's a toponym.

One sixteenth-century lexicographer, perhaps hungry while contemplating his painful big-toe joint, declared the *bunion* an *oignon du pied*, "onion of the foot." *Bunions* were called *onions* in the seventeenth and eighteenth centuries. But etymologically, bunions and onions are not related. *Bunion* comes from Old French *buignon, buigne*, "bump on the head." Wrong end of the body? Presumably it's the word *bump* that counts in this transfer of meaning, not *head*.

The words *broccoli* (from Italian *broccolo*, "cabbage sprout," from Latin *brocchus*, "projecting") and *tomato* (from Nahuatl via Spanish) showed up in English in the seventeenth century. Could the food have been in the diet if the word for it wasn't in the language?

So far, we have answered both yes and no to that question.

Yes, people ate breakfast before they had the word *breakfast*, taproots before they had the word *carrot*, and pungent bulbs before they had the word *onion*. But in the case of coffee, tea, sugar, and many other comestibles, word and food arrived together, though the foreign words clearly changed at least a bit in the mouths of English speakers. Likewise with *tomato* (a "botanical fruit but culinary vegetable"; see *pepper*, p. 151). There was probably not much

time between the arrival of the glossy
red fruit/vegetable in the diet of some
English speakers and the word *tomato*
in their language.

What's cool about a radish is
the company it keeps, not so much in
the salad as in word history. **Radish**
comes from Old English *raedic,* ultimately from the Indo-European root
wrād-, meaning "root." This *wrād-* is the root
of the English words *root, radical* ("affecting
the fundamental nature of something,"
"departure from tradition"), and *deracinate*
("to uproot someone"), as well as *wort, rutabaga,* and *licorice.*

Licorice came into English via French and
Latin from Greek *glukurrhiza,* from *glukos,*
"sweet," and *rhiza,* "root."

Rutabaga was borrowed from Swedish *rota-
bagge,* meaning both "root" and "stumpy thing."

A **wort** is not a wart, of course, but an herb or plant (from Old
English *wyrt*). Some worts are edible, like colewort ("cabbage").
Many were formerly used medicinally, like gutwort (a purgative),

and some are still popular as a medicine, like ***St.-John's-wort***. This plant is named after Saint John the Baptist because it blooms around the time of his feast, June 24. (***Feast*** can mean a day devoted to a particular saint; it's from Latin *festa,* "joyous.") The butterwort, so named because it supposedly keeps cows in milk and the supply of butter endless, is carnivorous. This wort traps and eats insects.

Mushroom appears in English at the end of the fourteenth century, borrowed from Anglo-French *musherum* and central French *moisseron*. *Shroom* is a shortened form of *mushroom* that refers especially to hallucinogenic mushrooms containing psilocybin. Presumably not part of tonight's salad.

The *toad* (from Old English *tādige*) has had a bad rep for ages. This amphibian was often considered poisonous—and sometimes was—so it's not surprising that *toadstool* mainly referred to poisonous mushrooms. *Toady,* from *toadeater* and meaning "a sycophant," came from the servile nature of the man who assisted a quack by pretending to eat a toad and then be cured by the quack's medicine. (*Quack* is probably from a Dutch word, *quackensalver,* from *quacken,* "to prattle," and *salf,* "salve.") To *smoke toad* means to get high on a substance derived from Sonoran Desert toads. They are very poisonous, but when the toxin is milked from the toad and vaporized, the resulting crystal is a nontoxic and powerful hallucinogen.

Raw-but-Marinated Foods

Some foods straddle the boundary between raw and cooked. For example, *marinating* a fish in acidic liquid breaks down its molecular structure. It *denatures* (*de,* "reversing," plus *nature*) the food. (*Marinate* comes from Italian *marinare,* "pickle in brine.") But marinated fish is still raw. It hasn't been cooked with heat, so any parasites present are not killed, yet it has been transformed—softened and flavored. The appetizer **ceviche** (probably from Quechuan *siwichi,* "fresh or tender fish") is typically defined as fish "cooked" in lime or other citrus juice—thus denatured.

Also not quite cooked, Ethiopian **kitfo** is a spicy minced beef that's raw but served warm. In the Amharic language, it's *leb leb*, "warm, very lightly cooked, like a runny yolk." On request, you can have it *betam leb leb* ("very warmed," or cooked).

Artichoke came into English in the sixteenth century from Italian *articiocco*, from Spanish Arabic *al-ḵaršūfa*. An artichoke looks like a thistle and sounds like something that might get stuck in your throat, but when the heart is softened and flavored by marinating, it makes a tasty addition to many dishes.

Uni, Japanese for "sea urchin," refers to the spiny creature's edible "roe," though more specifically, this part of the urchin consists of gonads, both ovaries and testes. *Uni* is eaten raw, sometimes served as **sashimi** (meaning "pierce body," probably referring to the slicing that's part of preparation), with a dipping sauce like wasabi, or as sushi with vinegared rice. Both the vinegared rice and dipping sauces can slightly "cook" a raw food, in the sense of breaking down molecules, but that bit of vinegar or a dip in the sauce isn't going to soften so much as add flavor to a raw gonad. *Uni* is sometimes a topping in a "warship roll" or **gunkanmaki,** which is sushi rice wrapped in nori (seaweed), forming a boatlike shape to hold toppings. Some say *uni* is strong-smelling, briny, and chewy; others say it's light and sweet.

Caviar is also at the boundary between raw and cooked due to the acidic process of pickling. The roe of sturgeon or other fish,

caviar comes from medieval Greek *khaviari* and may be traceable back to the Indo-European root *awi-,* "egg." One of its cognates is ***cockney,*** from "cock's egg." It's unlikely that anyone actually believed that a cock could lay an egg, although it was part of the myth of the cockatrice, a crocodile-like creature with a lethal gaze and breath that hatched from the egg of a cockerel (young male chicken). *Cockney* also meant a "pampered child" in Middle English and came to mean a "puny or affected person." It might then have been applied to any city-dweller, then to a person born in East London, then to the dialect of that area.

Everyone speaks a dialect, a variety of a language that suggests something about a person's background, and all dialects have subjective judgments attached to them. Cockney has been called low class and also very cool. Cockney is famous for rhyming slang: *bees and honey* means "money," *loaf of bread* means "head," *rub-a-dub* means "pub," and so on. Often the rhyming word is omitted, so one would say only *loaf* to mean "head." As with all lingos, you have to be in the know to understand.

What's in a name? Reputation, cultural values, ideas about what a food means. *Caviar* and *uni* connote expensive delicacies, perhaps more expensive than if they were called cock's eggs and urchin gonads.

Steak and Other Food on the Grill

Words related to cooked things often suggest growth. *Cook* comes from Old English *cōc,* from Latin *coquus,* and goes back to the Indo-European root *pek(w)-,* "to cook, ripen." This root gave us, among many other words, *biscuit* ("twice cooked" or "twice baked"); **ricotta** ("recooked," because it's made by heating the whey left over from producing other cheese or food); *apricot* (from Spanish Arabic *albarqūq,* "the apricot," in turn from Latin *praecoquum,* variant of *praecox,* "early ripening," because the apricot ripens before other fruits in the garden); and *precocious* (also from Latin *praecoquere*). Precocious kids aren't precooked, as the literal Latin might suggest; they simply ripen before other kids.

Here are some terms pertaining to foods often cooked on an open flame.

Shish kebab comes via Armenian from Turkish *şiş*, "skewer," and *kebap*, "roast meat." **Steak,** from Norse *stei, steikja*, "to roast on a spit," also refers to a method of cooking, though etymologically, it isn't necessarily meat that's roasted.

A **sirloin** is a cut of beef from above the loin (from French, *surlonge, sur,* "over," "above," and *longe,* "loin"). The word's history has nothing to do with knighting, though the fanciful pseudo-etymologies are fun — Henry VIII or some other monarch being amazed by a glorious hunk of meat and dubbing it "Sir Loin."

A **tenderloin** is a choice cut of meat as well as a choice assignment for a bribable policeman who would then turn a blind eye to crime. (On *bribe* as a piece of bread, see p. 53.) The story of bribing police may be apocryphal, but in the nineteenth century, Tenderloin was a district in New York City that was indeed full of corruption. A seedy but exciting and culturally vibrant district in San Francisco is also called the Tenderloin. Many notable people have lived and worked in the Bay Area's Tenderloin District, among them Dashiell Hammett, famous for his **hard-boiled** detective fiction, like *The Maltese Falcon,* characterized by gritty realism and unsentimental tough talk.

A ***buccaneer*** is a stolid, hard-boiled type—more specifically, a pirate plundering ships along the Atlantic Coast of the Americas in the seventeenth century. These buccaneers were Europeans in the West Indies who, in addition to exploring and plundering, smoked and cooked their meat on a *boucan,* a "frame for curing and cooking meat." They were following the practice of many Indigenous peoples. The word *buccaneer* came into English from French *boucanier,* from *boucan,* and ultimately from *mukem,* "frame," in the Tupi language of Brazil. Today, a buccaneer is a daring, possibly reckless person, especially in business.

Barbecue also comes from a word for a meat-drying frame. *Barbecue* was borrowed into English in the seventeenth century from Spanish *barbacoa,* probably from the Caribbean Arawakan word *barbacoa,* meaning "wooden frame for sleeping on and for drying food." *Barbecue* does not come from French *barbe à queue,* "beard to tail," despite sound similarities and popular belief.

If you prefer fish to steak, barbecue up some ***halibut.*** *Butt* was the name of a flatfish, probably the same fish we now call *flounder. Haly* means "holy"—the fish is a "holy butt" because it was often eaten on holy days in the Middle Ages. This fish was also made into a savory pie called, you guessed it, ***butt torte.***

Or throw ***salmon*** on the *barbie* (an Australian shortening of

barbecue and also derogatory slang for a mindless, conventionally pretty woman, from Barbie doll). Salmon was called *laex* in Old English (pronounced "lacks"). During the thirteenth century, the Old English word was replaced with a French/Latin word, as happened with many food terms. In this case, *laex* lost out to Anglo-Norman *saumoun,* from Latin *salmōn.*

By the mid-twentieth century, *laex* was back. A Yiddish cognate of the Old English word for *salmon* entered English — **lox** or *laks,* "smoked salmon"; so did the Scandinavian word **gravlax,** "dry-cured salmon." *Grav* means "trench" or "grave" and refers to the method of curing fish by burying it in the ground with salt and herbs.

The English word *grave* comes from the Indo-European root *g(w)erǝ-*, "heavy." Besides *gravlax*, descendants include *gravid* (meaning "pregnant," from Latin *gravis*, "burdened, heavy"), *guru* (Sanskrit, "esteemed"), and *charivari*, from Greek *karēbaria*, "head-heaviness," "headache."

A *charivari* or, in the English form of the word, *shivaree* is a mocking serenade involving yelling and banging on pots on the occasion of a wedding, the serenaders hoping to receive food and drink. Insofar as mockery makes light of something momentous, *shivaree* seems almost the opposite of "heavy," just as *grave* (burial place) and *gravid* (pregnant) seem near opposites. But words deriving from the same ancestor may end up with opposite meanings for any of the myriad reasons that affect semantic change, including cultural views.

For fun and insight into changing cultural views on gender, compare the changes over the past four hundred years in the meanings of *husband* and *housewife* (from which we get *hussy*), *governor* and *governess*, and *mister* and *mistress*. Why do the female-gendered terms take on negative meanings or become trivialized or sexualized?

One might say, with tongue in cheek, that the **codfish** became sexualized. The origin of *cod* possibly comes from Old English *cod(d)*, meaning "bag" or "pod." By the fifteenth century, if not before, *cod* meant "scrotum," as in the word *codpiece*. This decorative, pouch-like article of clothing was attached to a man's close-fitting hose, accentuating the privates. (Think of Hans Holbein's portrait of Henry VIII standing with legs apart, big codpiece almost dead center.) It wasn't a short-lived *fad* (from *fiddle-faddle*). The codpiece fashion lasted from about 1400 to 1600 and may now be returning. Various designers have included an outfit with a codpiece in runway shows.

When the codpiece was rising in popularity in the Renaissance, the word for this clothing accessory became a euphemism for *penis* (from Latin *pēnis*, "tail," "penis"). *Penis* is related to *penicillin*, from *penicill-*, "tail- or brush-like," referring to the appearance of the penicillium mold. From fish to fashion to lifesaving medicine — a far-reaching web of words.

If you're a *nimrod*, in the old sense of the word, meaning a "great hunter" (from Hebrew *Nimrod*, in Genesis 10), perhaps you've bagged a ***partridge*** as your contribution to the food roasting on the spit. This short-tailed game bird makes a whirring noise when startled, and ages ago, a Greek-speaking person called the bird *perdik* (or variant form of the word), from *perdesthai*, "to fart," and the name stuck. The name "farting fowl" didn't make it less desirable as a game bird or stop the word from being borrowed again and again, with its original meaning no doubt obscured,

A fashionable codpiece

from Greek to Latin to French to English. The word came into Middle English around 1300 from French *partrich.*

To increase a partridge's juiciness, you might want to **bard** it (cover the breast with bacon) or **lard** it (put strips of bacon under the skin). *Lard* comes from Latin *lardum,* "fat," and *bard* from French *barde,* meaning "warhorse's armor," from Arabic *barda'a,* "padded saddle." Not to be confused with *bard* meaning "poet," which was borrowed into English from Scottish Gaelic *bàird.*

In a Pot

Early hunter-gatherers began cooking in pots more than ten thousand years ago. After figuring out how to make pottery that could resist heat, they boiled wild grains and leafy plants. People still throw grains and plants and meat into a pot, cook them together, and call the result (among other things) **stew.**

Stew comes from Old French *estuve,* "to heat in steam," from Greek *tuphos,* "smoke, steam." *Stews* also meant "public baths" and "brothels" in early modern English. The connotations of the word *stew* tend to be negative when pertaining to humans (*Let him stew in his own juices* means "Let him worry, suffer anxiety") but positive when pertaining to cuisine. Still, some names for stews, even though the food is delicious, are strange or notable.

Many lovers of goat stew in the United States prefer not to say the word *goat*. They use *chevon* to indicate the meat used in the stew. *Chevon* is a blend of the French words *chèvre*, "goat," and *mouton*, "sheep." The term was coined in the 1920s by a trade association and has been adopted by the U.S. Department of Agriculture.

GOAT, the informal term meaning "greatest of all time," is an *acronym* (from Greek *akron*, "end or tip," and *onuma*, "name"). The term was first associated with Muhammad Ali and is usually used to describe great athletes and musicians. It has increasingly broadened to other domains.

An unusual name for a stew is *olla padrida*, from Spanish *olla*, "stew," from Latin *olla*, "cooking pot," and from *padrido*, "rotten." Why is this tasty, spicy vegetable and meat stew called "rotten"? An eighteenth-century explanation was that the word implied meat cooked until it had fallen to pieces. Whatever the reason — and likely there isn't one, other than tradition — the term isn't derogatory.

Consider also the case of *potpourri,* which centuries ago was the name of a stew made of different kinds of meat. Its literal meaning is "rotten pot," from French *pourri,* "rotten." Since the seventeenth century, *potpourri* has also referred to a mix of dried flowers and spices used for its good scent — for example, to freshen one's drawers (meaning one's undies or the place they're kept in or both). Just don't think of the etymology, and all will be well with that "rotten pot" of flowers next to your underwear.

Many stews have names that also mean "a jumble or potpourri." The word **bouillabaisse,** for example, refers to a fish stew made of five or sometimes six kinds of fish and seasoned with onions, herbs, and saffron; it can also mean a mixture or mess of things, as in "a bouillabaisse of odds and ends." The word *bouillabaisse* comes from Occitan (spoken in Provence) *boui-abaisso,* "boil" and "lower" (possibly meaning "simmering").

Paella, saffron-flavored rice with chicken, seafood, and vegetables, is cooked and served in a large shallow pan. The word *paella* comes from Spanish *paella,* but it's an old word going back to Catalan, to Old French, and to Latin *patella,* meaning "shallow dish" or "pan." *Paella,* like other meals-in-a-pot, refers to a miscellany or mixture, as in "his closet was a *paella* of designer clothes and old hand-me-downs."

One more example: **salmagundi,** a dish of chopped meat,

anchovies, eggs, and onions, also means a general mixture or a miscellaneous gathering of things (from French but of unknown origin before that).

A Few More Meals-in-a-Pot

Bibimbap is a popular one-dish meal of rice, vegetables, and fried meat topped with a raw or cooked egg. The word comes from Korean *pibimbap* (*pibim,* "to mix," and *pap,* "rice").

Jollof (or *jollof rice*) is a West African stew made with meat or fish, chili peppers, and rice, from Jollof, variant of Wolof, a language spoken in Senegal, Gambia, and elsewhere. *Jollof* is also called *benachin,* meaning "one pot," in Wolof.

Pho, made with beef-bone stock, sliced beef or chicken, noodles, spices, and often other ingredients as well, comes from Vietnamese *phở,* perhaps from French *feu,* as in *pot-au-feu,* "pot on the fire."

Ragout, a highly seasoned stew originally made of mutton and now sometimes of other meat, comes from French *ragoûter,* "revive the taste of," ultimately from Latin *gustus,* "taste." *Ragout* and *gusto* come from the same parent word.

Tzimmes comes from Yiddish for "fuss," as in "Why are you

making such a *tzimmes* over that?" It's a stew made with sweetened vegetables, fruit, and knaidel, or potato dumplings.

A veggie often found in stews (and also eaten alone), *potato* is a Caribbean loanword from the sixteenth century. It came via Spanish from the Caribbean Taino *batata*, "sweet potato." A ***spud*** is a short, narrow spade for digging. It's a Middle English word (possibly related to Old English *spadu*, "spade") that came to mean *potato* in the nineteenth century, perhaps by association with the tool, if indeed potatoes were dug with it (not much evidence for that). The origin of *spud* is a bit of a mystery.

Like potatoes, ***taros*** are often found in a single-pot meal. This edible starch originated in the Pacific islands but has been grown throughout the tropics and elsewhere (Nigeria is the biggest producer). In the Philippines, *sinigang*, made with taro, pork, beef, shrimp or fish, and other ingredients, is called a national stew. In Lebanon, taro, known as *kilkass*, is used in a popular winter stew made with lentils. In Jamaica, the leaves of taro (usually called *coco, cocoyam*, or *dasheen*) are used to make pepper pot soup. The word *taro* comes from the Maori language of New Zealand or, alternatively, from Tahitian and came into English in the eighteenth century.

Legumes are often part of the stew jumble, swapping juices with the other ingredients (to paraphrase Huckleberry Finn). From

Latin *legere,* which means "to read, choose, pick, gather," a *legume* is a plant whose seeds come in a pod. In light of the "picking and gathering" involved in harvesting legumes—such as lima beans, fava beans, kidney beans, black beans, chickpeas (see Cicero's nose, p. 100), lentils (meaning "lens"; see p. 108), peas, and peanuts—the derivation of *legume* from *legere* makes sense.

But what about the other meaning of *legere,* "to read"? Reading is like harvesting. The brainwork, one might say, involves picking out words and gathering meanings. *Legere* is also part of the etymology of *intellect* and *intelligent,* from Latin *intelligere* (variant of *intellegere*), meaning "to read between," or "to choose between, to discern." If intelligence is a matter of being able to

discern the best choices, the connection between *legume* and *intelligence* may not be as strange as it seems. Both involve picking, gathering, discerning, making choices. And yet it's good to remember that etymology can trace but not explain the vagaries of semantic change.

Off the Menu: They're Both Full of Beans

The Greek philosopher Pythagoras (circa 580-500 BCE) had a problem with legumes, notably the fava bean. Known for his theorem about right triangles, he's also known for his diet. He believed it was wrong to eat animals and abstained from eating meat and fish, but he did not eat beans either. Over the centuries, many explanations for this bean taboo have been offered, from physical discomfort to the supposed fetus-like look of fava beans, but if there ever was an explicit reason, it's now lost.

Pythagoras abstained from fava beans; Hannibal Lecter famously ate them. In the movie *The Silence of the Lambs*, Lecter says with relish (and a horrible sucking noise) that he ate a man's liver with fava beans and a nice Chianti. Definitely not a follower of Pythagoras.

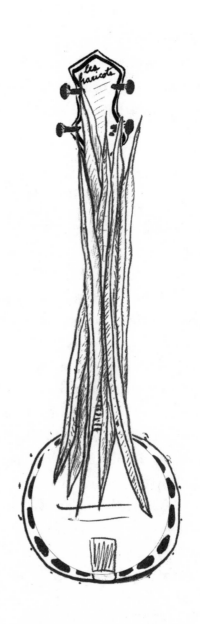

Green beans, or *string beans,* bring us away from the scary Hannibal Lecter and to the great music called *zydeco.* It's dance music that originated in Louisiana and is often played on an accordion and a guitar or other stringed instrument. The word probably comes from a Louisiana Creole form of French *les haricots,* "[green] beans." The word gives a new sense to the idea of stringed instruments.

Nuts

Let us now praise the nut. Good for the heart, brain, and gut, loaded with vitamins, minerals, antioxidants, fiber, and "good" fats that may lower "bad" LDL cholesterol, nuts are a fine choice for dessert, especially if you don't want any more sugar. And some nuts have notable etymologies.

Walnut comes from Old English *walhhnutu,* "foreign" (*walh*) and "nut" (*hnutu*), meaning the nut of the Celts or Romans. Walnuts were cultivated on the Continent before they were introduced into Britain, where the *hazelnut* (from Old English *haesel,* "hazel tree") was more common. The Anglo-Saxons also used the Old English word *walh* or *wealh,* "foreign," to refer to Celtic people, including the Welsh. But the Celts were in Britain long before the Angles and Saxons (who arrived in the sixth century CE), so the

designation *Welsh* was an instance of newcomers, indeed foreigners, referring to people they'd conquered or pushed into the hinterlands as foreign.

Some walnut eaters claim that the nut is not only good for the brain but resembles it—at least, the two-lobed walnut may look like a brain if you let your imagination wander. Another nut-brain connection involves the two almond-shaped parts of the brain called the *amygdalae,* which derives, like our word *almond,* from Greek *amugdalē,* meaning (what else?) "almond." (See also "Food Words from Body Parts," p. 107). Almonds contain a small amount of cyanide, not enough to hurt a person, but bitter almonds (an inedible form of almond used to make oil) contain a larger amount and should be avoided.

Another name for the *hazelnut* is the ***filbert***—an eponymous nut named after a saint. Saint Philibert was a seventh-century French abbot whose feast day (dedicated to celebrating a saint) is August 20. Celebrating Philibert thus overlapped with celebrating the bounty of the harvest, including the first ripening of filberts. Though it may seem a far-fetched derivation, it's certainly possible that a saint became associated with a nut.

Chestnut comes from early modern English *chesten,* "chestnut," from Latin *castanea,* "chestnut." The word *nut* was added to *chesten* in the eighteenth century, so the word is redundant, "chestnut-nut." *Chestnut* can be traced back to Greek *kastanea,* an ancient region in Asia Minor on the Black Sea.

Our word *castanets*—concave pieces of wood clicked rhythmically with the fingers—also goes back to the Greek *kastanea* (via Spanish *castaña*, "chestnut"), because castanets supposedly resemble chestnuts. When the word is used figuratively, *chestnut* means a stale joke or anything repeated too often. "An apple a day keeps the doctor away" is an old chestnut.

The popularity of some nuts can be measured by the spread of the nut's name. The word **pistachio** appears (in varying forms) in a great many languages across Europe and the Middle East: Greek (*pistakion*); Latin (*pistacium*); virtually all Romance languages, including French (*pistace*); Swedish (*pistacie*); Dutch (*pistache*) and other Germanic languages; and Farsi (*pistah*). The word probably ultimately comes (via Persian *pistah*) from Aramaic *pistqā*.

The pistachio tree is a desert plant and can live as long as three hundred years. When ripe, the nuts pop open—audibly. Pistachios contain *urushiol* (from Japanese *urushi*, "lacquer"), an oily substance that can be an irritant and cause allergic reactions; it's the same irritant found in cashews and poison ivy. Consumed in moderation, pistachios are a safe nut with health benefits like lowering the risk of heart disease (per the U.S. FDA 2003 statement), and they may promote good sleep too.

Some people eschew the cashew because of the urushiol (especially in raw cashews) and the relatively high oxalate content that might, in large doses, affect the kidneys. Nevertheless, eaten in moderation, cashews provide many of the health benefits of other nuts. **Cashew** comes via Portuguese from Tupi, *acaju* or *caju*. Tupi, an Indigenous language formerly spoken in Brazil, is now extinct.

Pie

If your sweet tooth is acting up after dinner, consider the fruit discussed in "Breakfast" (pp. 54–64) or try **durian,** a fruit considered delicious even though it has a somewhat peculiar smell. The fruit comes from Malaysia, and the word comes from Malay, *dori,* "thorn."

 Dessert derives from French *desservir,* "to remove what has been served, to clear (the table)." *Desert,* meaning "dry, arid land," comes from Latin *dēsertum,* "something left, waste." This is also the source of the verb *desert,* accent on the second syllable, meaning "to leave, or forsake."

 And then there's the word *deserts,* also with the accent on the second syllable and virtually always used in the plural, as in *just deserts,* meaning "what a person deserves." The word *deserts* is related to *deserve,* both deriving from Old French *deservir,* "to deserve," from Latin *dēservīre,* "to earn or merit something by service," "to serve well."

People getting their *just deserts* might have to eat **humble pie.**
The expression *humble pie* comes from a pun on *humble* (from
Latin *humilis,* "low, lowly," from *humus,* "ground") and the word
umbles, meaning "offal." Offal consists of the entrails and inner
organs of an animal. If you must eat offal, and if you consider it
inferior food (not everyone does), you're [*h*]*umbling* yourself (with
or without the *h* pronounced).

The word *pie* probably comes from *magpie,* the bird that col-
lects all sorts of objects, especially shiny ones, and puts them in its
nest. *Magpie,* in turn, comes from a woman's name, *Magot* (nickname for Margery or Margaret), plus *pie,* which comes from Latin
pīca, "magpie" (related to *pīcus,* "woodpecker").

But why are birds mixed up in the etymology of *pie?* The
semantic connection between *magpie* and the food we call *pie*—
the baked, usually round, sweet- or savory-filled pastry—depends,
one speculates, on the diverse ingredients needed to make a
pie. Or, better yet, the connection depends on the magical transformation that results from combining ingredients. The magpie
combines improbable objects and gets a decorated nest, a great lure
for a mate. A person measures, shifts, rolls out, fills, crimps edges,
bakes, and gets a tasty pastry.

Note the improbable transformations—at least from a playful
word-nerd's point of view—that produce the *rhubarb pie.* Its
main ingredient is "barbarous and foreign," according to

rhubarb's etymology (Greek *rha,* "rhubarb," and *barbarum,* "foreign," "barbarous").

The pie is *garbled*—that is, the spices in it have been separated from dirt (from *garble,* "to get rid of refuse by putting through a sieve"). One of these spices consists of nails—*cloves,* from *clou de girofle,* "nail of the gillyflower." Another possibly unappetizing spice, if we go by its etymology, comes from the scrotum of a deer—*musk,* etymologically also part of *nutmeg* (see discussion in "Breakfast," pp. 39, 59–60). And the leaves of the rhubarb plant are poisonous. Nevertheless, this barbarous, partly poisonous, garbled, musky, nail-filled pie is gloriously sweet and zingy.

Rhubarb is also baseball slang for a heated dispute and theater jargon for actors mumbling in the background, pretending to talk but only repeating "rhubarb" over and over.

Other spices contributing to the transformation that results in a rhubarb pie include cinnamon and ginger. The word history of these and virtually any spice reveals, among other things, the early global spread of these desirable commodities. Cinnamon is native to Sri Lanka, Bangladesh, and Myanmar and was being traded as early as 2000 BCE. The English word *cinnamon* comes, via French and Latin, from Greek *kinnamon,* from a Semitic origin (compare the Hebrew word for cinnamon: *quinnāmōn*).

Ginger originated in Maritime Southeast Asia and started its spread around the world about 3000 BCE. The word *ginger*

probably goes back to *singivera,* from Pali, the ancient Indic language akin to Sanskrit. Ultimately the word goes back to Tamil and Malayalam, which are Dravidian (non-Indo-European) languages spoken in Southeast Asia. The word appears in a great many languages. In Hellenistic Greek, *ginger* is *zingiberis;* in classical Latin *zingiberi;* in Arabic *zanjabil* (found in the Koran, 76:17); in Irish *sinséar;* in Chinese *jiāng;* in Vietnamese *gừng.* In Old English, the spice was called *gingifer;* in Middle English it was *giniure* or *gingeuir* (influenced by French and Anglo-Norman forms); and eventually in early modern English, it was called *ginger.*

Ginger, gingerly, and *gingivitis* are not related etymologically, despite the similarity in form and sound. The adverb *gingerly,* meaning "daintily, carefully," comes via French from Latin *genitus,* "(well-) born," and goes back to the Indo-European root *genə,* "to give birth." This productive root has yielded *gentle, generous, gender, genre, genus, gene, engender, genius, jaunty,* and many other words in English, French, and other languages. But it didn't give us *gingivitis,* "inflammation of the gums," which can be traced back to Latin *gingivae,* "gums," but no further.

Having detoured around the world to spice up a pie, we return to tarts. A *tart* (or *tarte*) is often defined as an open pastry containing a filling (from Old French *tarte* or medieval Latin *tarta,* of unknown origin), so it's sometimes indistinguishable from pie. What about tarts that aren't food? *Tart* meaning a "sharp, possibly acidic taste" or a "cutting, biting tone" comes from Old English *teart,* meaning "harsh." Although it sounds identical to *tart* meaning "pie," the two words are unrelated. A third *tart* refers to a woman who is a prostitute or considered to behave in a sexually provocative way. It's probably derived, ironically, from *sweetheart.*

Pie- or Cake-Like Desserts That Amuse the Mouth and Mind

Clafouti is a custard-and-cherry dessert with a pancake-like batter that's baked instead of fried. *Clafouti* is from Old French *claufir* or *clafir,* "to stuff." The French word seems to be a blend of the Latin expression *clāvō figere* ("pierce with a nail," from *clāvō,* "with a nail" and *figere,* "attach, pierce") and the French word *clafir.* A popular explanation for the name *clafouti* says that the cherries resemble nails or studs that pierce the batter. That explanation depends mainly on the Latin part of the blend, *clāvō figere,* but the French word *clafir* bears more investigating. *Cla,* "nail," seems unproblematic. But lexicographers say the second part of *clafir* comes from *fouti,* in turn from *foutre* (which English speakers might call the French F-word). *Foutre* has many meanings besides "have sex with," including "throw, put carelessly," and perhaps the dessert is simply "thrown together." If so, *clafouti* is no less tasty for being hasty (and having a slight whiff of the salacious?).

From an Old French dessert to two old British puddings (in British English, **pudding** is often a generic term for dessert):

Spotted dick is a steamed pudding made of suet with raisins or currants. *Dick* comes from the nickname for Richard. (Why Dick and not Tom or Harry? Who knows.) **Unspotted dick** has no raisins. **Treacle dick** is made with treacle sauce, a molasses-like syrup that's a byproduct of refining sugar. *Treacle* also of course means "cloying" and "saccharine." The word derives ultimately from Greek *thēriakē,* "an antidote against venom." Over the centuries, *treacle* has gone from lifesaving medicine to phony sentiment.

Eton mess is made with whipped cream, meringue, and strawberries or other fruit. It's traditionally associated with Eton College, the famous school near Windsor founded in 1440.

And on to old American desserts:

Grunt is a pudding-like dessert (*pudding* in the U.S. sense of "a custard-like dessert"). The word *pudding* probably comes from Anglo-Norman *bodeyn,* "sausage," "stuffed entrails." (Not very dessert-like.) Making *grunt* requires many steps, including folding foil, tying with string, putting vessels inside vessels. Here are the main steps: covering berries with biscuit dough, placing the mixture in a mold or soufflé dish, putting the dish in a Dutch oven, filling it half full of boiling water, and simmering. Why the name *grunt?* Perhaps because it involves lots of "grunt work" or because it's humble, like GI "grunts," who are low-ranking soldiers. Probably the name comes from the noise the pudding makes when plated. Apparently, the grunt grunts when it's inverted and urged out of its mold.

The word *grunt* is from Old English *grunnettan,* "to grunt," probably of imitative origin. The Old English word has also given us *gruntle,* meaning "to grunt" (said of swine since at least the fifteenth century) and also "to grumble, murmur, complain" (said of people since at least the sixteenth century). The adjective *disgruntled,* "chagrined," "in a bad mood," first appeared in the seventeenth century (said of people, not swine), and in the early twentieth century, people could be *gruntled,* meaning "in a good mood." *Gruntled* is a back-formation, almost always used humorously.

A **cobbler** is a deep-dish fruit pie with a top crust. The crust is now often made with biscuit dough (flour, sugar, butter, milk, baking powder, with many variants) rather than pie crust. The dessert's name perhaps refers to the idea of the dessert being "cobbled" or pieced together.

Cobbler, meaning a person who patches or makes shoes, is of unknown origin. The verb *cobble* is probably a back-formation from the noun. Other back-formations of this sort include *edit* from *editor; televise* from *television; burgle* from *burglar.*

The words *cherry, pea, sherry,* and *caper* are also back-formations but of a different sort. They're not verbs formed from an existing noun but nouns formed from certain singular nouns being shortened, losing their *se* or *s* ending because they were misunderstood as plurals. Thus, *cherise* became *cherry*, *sherris* became *sherry* (see p. 105), *pease* became *pea*, and *caperis* became *caper* (not the verb meaning to skip and dance but the pickled bud of a shrub used to flavor food, from Latin *capparis*). *Cherise, sherris,* and *caperis* were borrowed into English from French, Spanish, and Latin, which might explain the impulse to lop off a foreign-sounding *s* on a singular word. But even a native word like *pease* (from Old English *pise*, plural *pisan*) could sound wrong as a singular in early modern English.

The word *za*, from *pizza*, shows a recent variation on the practice of back-formation, with the first part of the word dropped rather than the end.

Off the Menu: Backside Back-Formations

Pants is a shortened form of *pantaloons*, formerly meaning "men's tight-fitting breeches" and named after the sixteenth-century Italian comic character Pantalone, who wore such breeches. The already-shortened word *pants* is getting shorter in the United States in certain circles. Clothing advertisers, some fashionistas, those feeling a slight grammar-reality disconnect when using a plural verb to talk about a singular item — for these people, *pant* is now the preferred word for "an article of clothing worn on the lower half of the body with separate covering for each leg." *Pant* has been in use for a century or so but hasn't yet displaced the more common "pair of pants" to denote the singular. The word *trousers* is undergoing a similar back-formation process, except the word was made longer before being shortened. *Trousers* was borrowed in the sixteenth century as *trouse*, from Scottish Gaelic *triubhas*, a singular noun meaning "close-fitting clothing for the legs." But instead of lopping off the *se*, English speakers add an *r*, perhaps influenced by *drawers*. Nowadays, one often hears the shortened form *trou* (pronounced "trow" as in *trowel*), though usually in a humorous context or expression (*drop trou*).

Baba, or **baba au rhum,** "rum cake," is a yeast cake made with eggs, milk, and butter, soaked in a syrup made with rum, and traditionally baked as individual servings in tall cylindrical molds but now also in a round ring mold. *Baba* comes via French from Polish *babka,* a diminutive of *baba,* meaning (in many Slavic languages) "old woman" or "grandmother."

Also soaked in liquor is the rich cake called ***tiramisu:*** espresso and mascarpone cheese between alcohol-saturated layers of sponge cake. The name comes from Italian *tira mi su,* "pick me up."

Frangipane, a cake or pastry filled with almond-flavored cream, is an eponym, named after the seventeenth-century Marquis Frangipani, who created a perfume from a shrub now called frangipani. The perfume was subsequently used to flavor the almond cream.

Off the Menu: A Sweet Deal

Some words of old have narrowed in meaning. *Starve* used to mean "to die," then came to mean specifically "to die of hunger." *Wade* meant "to move" before it came to mean "move through water." And *hound,* formerly meaning "dog" in general, came to mean specifically the hunting breeds we call hounds. *Junket,* however, has expanded in meaning over time. The word derives from French *jonquette,* "a sweet made with boiled milk," and from medieval Latin *joncata,* "a kind of soft cheese." In English it meant "sweetened curds," then "any sweetened dish," then "a feast." It now means a sweet deal in the form of a trip paid for by others — often employers or taxpayers.

For those who want something cold for dessert, there's sorbet, a frozen dessert, formerly an iced drink, usually made from syrup, fruit juice, and sugar. The word **sorbet** came into English in the late sixteenth century from French *sorbet,* from Italian *sorbetto,* in turn from Turkish *şerbet* and Persian *šerbet,* ultimately going back to Arabic *šarba,* "a drink," and *šariba,* "to drink." *Sherbet,* made from iced syrup, sometimes with milk added, shares a similar history, coming into English about the same time as *sorbet,* ultimately from Arabic *shariba,* "to drink."

For those who want something cold and creamy with a cherry on top: a **sundae.** The story goes that Charles Platt, inventor of ice cream novelties and owner of a pharmacy in Ithaca, New York, served an ice cream dish with a topping to a pastor on a Sunday in 1892, calling the treat an "ice-cream Sunday." It's not clear when, why, or by whom the spelling was changed to *sundae*— perhaps it made a more notable trademark or was less likely to offend some people if it was not so clearly connected to a day of worship. Pastor and Platt were apparently pleased with the treat, and sundae-eaters ever since have agreed the concoction is blessedly yummy.

For those who want something both hot and cold, there's the coffee affogato: espresso poured over very cold ice cream, a sippable kind of sundae that one can also dig into with a spoon. *Affogato* means "drowned" in Italian, much like the ice cream in the

espresso here. For coffee lovers, the shiver and thrill of cold meeting hot is—in the parlance of today—to die for.

And for those in a hurry: a ***Milky Way.*** This candy bar bears the name of our galaxy, the "Milky Way," named in turn for a band of light that looks from the Earth like a streak of milk arching across the sky. The candy bar's name also indicates the etymology of the word *galaxy:* it comes from Greek *galaxias* (*galakt-*), "milk," and *kuklos,* "circle, vault, arched roof."

Frank Mars, who invented the Milky Way in 1923, supposedly

wasn't thinking of the night sky when he named his candy bar but rather of milkshakes.

Showstoppers

Loosen the cummerbund of your tuxedo and make room for a showstopping dessert. The dinner jacket, by the way, that came to be known as a *tuxedo jacket*—formal but without tails—made an appearance at a country club in Tuxedo Park, New York, in the late nineteenth century, and the place-name (at least the Tuxedo part) stuck as the name of the jacket. The word *tuxedo* may come from the language of the Delaware First Nations as a place-name meaning "crooked river" or possibly as a reference to the wolf totem.

The showstopper dessert called **cherries jubilee** is made from sweet red cherries, sugar, lemon juice, butter, and kirsch, all boiled until syrupy; brandy is then added and set on fire, and finally the sauce is poured over ice cream, mousse, or cake. According to tradition, cherries jubilee was first made by the famous French chef Auguste Escoffier for Queen Victoria's Diamond Jubilee in 1897.

A *jubilee* is a special anniversary celebrating, for example, sixty years of a reign. The word comes from late Latin *jūbilaeus (annus)*, "(year) of jubilee," based on Hebrew *yōḇēl*, "ram's-horn trumpet."

In Jewish tradition, this trumpet was used every fifty years to proclaim the beginning of *jubilee,* a year of emancipation and restoration. In the Roman Catholic tradition, a jubilee year occurred every twenty-five years and granted (under certain conditions) remission from sins — that is, from the pains of atoning for them in purgatory.

On a lighter note (no apologies for puns), *jubilee* also means "lit" or "flambé," from French for "singed." A flaming dessert like cherries jubilee seldom fails to bring exclamations from guests, usually of delight, unless the one with the match stands too close and gets his eyebrows singed.

Dinner began with an amuse-bouche (a tidbit that "amuses the mouth"; see p. 133), and dinner now ends with a counterpart word that also calls attention to amusing the mouth — a **croquembouche** or *croque-en-bouche* ("[that which] crunches in the mouth"). This tall pyramid of puff pastries is wound around with sugary threads. Pluck off a pastry and bite it. The crunch and squish of caramel-encrusted cream-filled puffs amuse the mouth.

A croquembouche or any showstopper, especially a wedding cake, also amuses the eye. The sight of it is satisfying, and so is watching someone make it. Even a showstopper recipe — which always turns out to be a series of embedded recipes — amuses the mind. It's satisfying to read recipes. For those of us who are wowed and cowed by fancy concoctions, it's as fun to read the recipe as

to make it. Reading recipes means thinking about the promise of transformation — of ingredients becoming a dish and of words becoming food.

Recipe is the imperative form ("Take!") of the Latin verb *recipere,* "to receive or take." It was used in medieval and early modern times at the beginning of lists of ingredients for medical prescriptions: "*Recipe* two drams of cod oil…" or "*Recipe* honey with…" The word *recipe* was often abbreviated to ℞, an R with a line crossing its right leg. In modern usage, this abbreviation is usually printed *Rx* and has come to mean "prescription."

What's the recipe for a relaxing evening? Don your nightcap and read on…

6

Nightcaps

*Evening Drinks and End-of-the-Day
Thoughts About Food Language*

A *nightcap* used to mean headwear, a cap to keep one's noggin warm in bed. Now it's a drink, often hot, often alcoholic, to cap the day and keep one's insides toasty. Some people drink a noggin of *whiskey* as a nightcap. As noted in "Happy Hour" (p. 126), the word *whiskey* is from Scottish Gaelic *uisge beatha* or Irish Gaelic *uisce beathadh*, "water of life." *Noggin*, besides meaning a person's head, refers to a quantity of liquor (about a quarter of a pint) and the drinking cup that holds it. Origin of *noggin?* Nobody knows. But the first recorded instance of the word (in the sixteenth century) refers to a cup; a century later, it also meant an amount of liquor, and in the eighteenth century, *noggin* meaning "head" (so called because it looks like a round cup?) appeared as part of boxing slang.

Some want a snifter of brandy in the evening. Like a *noggin*, a *snifter* is both a smallish quantity and a drinking vessel, specifically a footed glass that's wide at the bottom and tapers to the top. *Snifter* may be imitative in origin and related to *sniff, sniffle, snuffle,* and *snort.* (Try saying that five times in a row.) *Brandy* comes from Dutch *brandewijin,* meaning "burned wine." Unlike the etymology of *whiskey* with its vast existential claim — it's the very "water of life" — *brandy*'s etymology indicates the more mundane matter of how it's made — through distillation, a process involving heating (hence "burned") and cooling.

A toddy consists of a distilled spirit, usually whiskey, with hot water, sugar or honey, and spices, but it was originally fermented palm sap, as its etymology suggests. The word comes from western Indian Marathi *tadi,* akin to Hindi *tari,* both meaning "palm wine." It goes back to a Dravidian language (see appendix), perhaps Telugu. English colonizers borrowed the word in the seventeenth century, during the early days of the East India Company (see p. 36). About the same time, they also borrowed *punch* (Hindi *panch,* from Sanskrit *pañca* and *pañcāmṛta,* "five nectars of the gods," referring to the drink's five ingredients, which were probably liquor, water, lemon juice, sugar, and spices).

A hot toddy has traditionally been considered medicinal and *soporific* ("sleepy-making," from Latin *sopor,* "sleep"). To promote sleep, some prefer a mug of **chamomile** tea (from Greek *khamaimēlon,* "earth-apple," because of the apple-like smell of the tea), or hot milk, or the fermented milk called **kefir.** The word comes from Russian *kefir* (same meaning as in English), ultimately from a non-Indo-European language in Eastern Europe, probably the Adyghe language.

Off the Menu: When Languages Go Extinct

Adyghe is one of two official languages (the other is Russian) of the Adyghe Republic, a country situated in the North Caucasus of Eastern Europe. Adyghe is spoken by about three hundred thousand people in Turkey, Jordan, Syria, Israel, and the United States. Nevertheless, in today's world of dominant languages swallowing smaller ones, Adyghe is in danger of extinction.

Before the end of this century, possibly half the world's seven thousand or so languages will be extinct. When languages disappear, some aspect of culture, however small, disappears as well — names of plants, flowers, and foods that can yield information about origins and uses. *Kefir's* possible derivation from the Adyghe words for "barrel" and "to make sour" suggests how this fermented-milk drink might have been made at one time — by the barrelful, like beer.

Kefir reminds us that English has been enriched with words from many languages, including non-Indo-European ones and endangered or extinct languages. The Caribbean Arawakan language Taino gave English the word *barbecue*. The Tupi language of Brazil is probably the source of *buccaneer*. Eastern Abenaki gave us *moose*, other Algonquian languages gave us *pone* and *hominy* (p. 65), and Hawaiian gave us *poi* (p. 13) and *luau* (p. 15). Taino and Tupi are extinct. Algonquian languages are endangered. Extensive efforts to keep Hawaiian alive — for example, by teaching it in school — have been effective, but it is still at risk.

Some nightcappers want a combination soothing-stimulating drink, like hot cocoa with a splash of Kahlúa. (*Cocoa,* an alteration of cacao, comes from Nahuatl *cacaua.* Kahlúa is a proprietary name for a coffee-flavored liqueur originally from Mexico.) The hot milk soothes, the small amount of caffeine in the cocoa stimulates, and the Kahlúa does both.

Or a soothing-stimulating drink like an ***Irish coffee.*** (*Coffee* comes via Turkish *kahveh,* from Arabic *qahwa;* see p. 28.) The word *Irish* comes from Old English *Ir,* possibly going back to the Indo-European root *peiə,* "swelling, fat, fertile." Besides the rich taste and the warmth of Irish coffee, the ritual-like method of making it is enjoyable: brewing strong coffee, adding it to whiskey and sugar in a tall glass with a handle, and carefully pouring heavy whipping cream over the back of a spoon into the glass.

Make another for a friend. Dim the lights, curl up on the couch, sip the coffee through the cream that sits on top, stream a movie…

Some want more—an *aphrodisiac,* "food, drink, or drug that arouses sexual desire," from Greek *aphrodisiakis,* from *Aphrodite,* goddess of love. (Her name in turn means "foam-born.") Aside from drugs and animal parts, like rhino tusks and pangolin scales, sought-after aphrodisiacs in the last few centuries have included virtually every spice, aromatic, and stimulating drink ever tried by English speakers, including nutmeg, ambergris, Rocky Mountain oysters (fried bull testicles), pot brownies, edibles (edible cannabis), coffee, tea, distilled spirits, and the spiced wine called **hippocras** or *ypocras.* (It may be named after the Greek physician Hippocrates, or it may be a form of an Old French drink called *boucras.*) For some would-be lovers, however, alcohol may both give and take away, first stimulating mind and body, then delivering a double whammy of drowsiness and fitful sleep.

Whatever nightcap is your *nectar* ("the drink of the gods," from Greek *nektar,* "overcoming death"), you may want a tasty tidbit to go with it, something rich and satisfying, like a big piece of blueberry pie à la mode. Yes, even though dinner wasn't long ago.

One explanation for the urge to eat is that ghrelin, a hormone produced mainly in the stomach and intestines, stimulates the brain, which then tells us to eat. (The word *ghrelin* was coined in the 1990s, from *gh,* for "growth hormone," *rel,* for "releasing," and *in. Hormone* comes from Greek *horman,* "impel, set in motion.") This hormonal belly-brain conversation increases appetite.

But appetite is complicated (*No kidding*, you say), because it may be aroused when a person isn't exactly hungry, or rather *is* hungry but not because the belly is empty. The craving may come from habit associated with circumstance (like relaxing with a friend and a late-night toddy), or seeing that pie, or the anticipated pleasure of eating. The possible connections between ghrelin and circumstance, between ghrelin and *anorexia* (Greek *an-*, "without," and *orexis*, "appetite"), and between ghrelin and hormonal imbalances that can lead to *pathophysiology* (Greek *pathos*, "suffering, disease") — these connections are still being sorted out.

How does appetite end? Another tricky question. One answer is that the hormone *leptin* (from Greek *leptós*, "thin") tells us when we're full, *satiated*, or have reached *satiety* (both words from Latin *satura*, "well-fed, replete," also meaning "seasoned stuffing" or "sausage"). When the words *satiated* and *satiety* entered English in the sixteenth century, they had a negative sense of overindulging in food and drink. They still sometimes imply excess, though *satiety* is usually neutral, particularly as a term used by researchers in talking about appetite's end.

All things considered, including late-night cravings, this ghrelin-leptin-ghrelin merry-go-round is worth the price of admission to the amusement park of the body. (That's ghrelin talking.) The rousing and satisfying of appetite day after day is potentially one of the great pleasures in life, even while it's fraught with complications.

Ghrelin and *leptin* (those rascals) are relatively recent additions to the language and probably not everyday words for many of us. What does common food talk tell us about our view of ourselves and others? To get this bigger view of food language, let's change the focus from the history of individual words to current ways of talking about food.

You Are What You Eat?

We often talk as if we're the sum of the protein, carbs, and fat we ate yesterday, and we define ourselves and others in terms of food: "I'm a vegan." "I'm an overeater." "I'm watching my weight." "She should consume more calcium." "Children should eat less sugar." "I'm fasting."

Our conventional food-metaphor expressions also show how we think about human behavior in terms of food. For example, we conceptualize the abstract idea of flattery by using butter. Flattery is "buttering up someone." We conceptualize the abstraction "living well" by mapping it onto eating meat. Living well is "living high off the hog" (some say "high on the hog")—eating the choicest cuts. What is a faulty argument? "Cherry-picking" the evidence, using only facts we like and ignoring those we don't. According to some cognitive linguists, these conceptual metaphors suggest that food is a very productive "source domain" for understanding abstractions.

Because these conventional expressions show entrenched ways of thinking, people mostly register only the abstract meaning. We

the proof's in the pudding

Sugarcoat

cooking the books

Voracious   toe beans

Sow Wild Oats   toast of the town

Not my cup of tea

recipe for success   Stud Muffin

The Spice of Life

Salad Days

Word Salad

It's all gravy

in Hog Heaven

in a nutshell

Pie in the sky   in a Pickle

Easy as pie   a tough nut to crack

Pigging Out   Pie hole

like putting lipstick on a pig

can and do stop to think about these expressions, however, and if we don't like them (does living well really mean eating pork?), we don't use them. Nevertheless, we often use food language to understand who and what we are and how we relate to others.

Food talk (and food writing) is always about more than food. It's about who's eating what, where the food comes from, who cooks it, who goes without. It's about how we're subject to appetite's demands but also capable of choosing. Humans sit at the top of the food chain, aware that we will someday be food for worms. We're part of nature as well as culture, turning food into muscle and waste but also into symbols—of divinity, family, memory, companionship, and love.

Appendix

Languages from Which English Has Borrowed Food Words

Adyghe, from Caucasus area of Eastern Europe; part of the Caucasian language family

Akan, Twi, Ewe, Igbo, Mande, Bantu, from Ghana, Nigeria, Angola, and members of the Niger-Congo language family

Algonquian languages, including **Eastern Abenaki,** originally spoken in Quebec and New England; **Lenape,** originally spoken in parts of Pennsylvania, New York, New Jersey, and Delaware; **Miami-Illinois,** formerly spoken in the midwestern U.S. and areas along the Mississippi; and **Ojibwe,** also called **Chippewa,** originally spoken in the region around Lake Superior

Amharic, from Ethiopia, part of the Afro-Asiatic language family

Arabic and **Hebrew,** from the Semitic language family

Dakota, originally spoken in the Upper Midwest of the U.S. and parts of Canada, belonging to the Siouan language family

French, Spanish, Italian, Portuguese, Latin, Norse, Dutch, German, Yiddish, Afrikaans, Russian, Celtic, Persian/ Farsi, Hindi, Urdu, Romani, Sanskrit—all members (though from different branches) of the Indo-European language family

Japanese, often called an isolate—unrelated to other languages— or, alternatively, part of the Japonic group, which includes the Ryukyuan languages of Ryukyu Island

Khmer and **Vietnamese,** from the Mon-Khmer family, part of the Austroasiatic group

Korean, considered by most linguists to be an isolate

Malay, from Malaysia, and **Hawaiian,** both Austronesian languages

Mandarin, Cantonese, and other forms of **Chinese,** from the Sino-Tibetan group

Nahuatl, from southern Mexico and Central America, part of the Uto-Aztecan language family

Quechua, a language family primarily from the Peruvian Andes

Taino, formerly spoken in the Antilles, of the Arawakan language family; said to be the first language Columbus and crew encountered in the New World

Tamil and other **Dravidian** languages, spoken in Sri Lanka and parts of India

Thai, part of the Kra-Dai group

Tupi, a branch of languages from the Tupi-Guarani group, from the Amazon River basin

Turkish, from the Turkic language family

Sources and Suggested Reading

FOR ETYMOLOGY

American Heritage Dictionary of Indo-European Roots. 3rd ed. Revised and edited by Calvert Watkins. Boston: Houghton Mifflin Harcourt, 2011.

American Heritage Dictionary of the English Language. 5th ed. Boston: Houghton Mifflin Harcourt, 2018. Also available at https://www.ahdictionary.com.

Dictionary of Old English: A to I. Edited by Angus Cameron, Ashley Crandell Amos, and Antonette diPaolo Healey. Toronto: Dictionary of Old English Project, 2007 (online access requires subscription).

Merriam-Webster Unabridged Dictionary. Continually updated at https://unabridged.merriam-webster.com/unabridged/.

Middle English Dictionary. Edited by Robert E. Lewis et al. Ann Arbor: University of Michigan Press, 1952–2001. Online edition in Middle English Compendium. Edited by Frances

McSparran et al. Ann Arbor: University of Michigan Library, 2000–2018. http://quod.lib.umich.edu.

New Oxford American Dictionary. 3rd ed. Edited by Angus Stevenson and Christine A. Lindberg. New York: Oxford University Press, 2010. https://doi.org/10.1093/acref/9780195392883.001.0001.

Oxford English Dictionary. 2nd ed. 20 vols. Oxford: Oxford University Press, 1989. Continually updated (requires a subscription).

Oxford Latin Dictionary. 2nd ed. Edited by P.G.W. Glare. Oxford: Oxford University Press, 2012.

ON LANGUAGE

Cambridge Encyclopedia of the English Language. 2nd ed. Edited by David Crystal. Cambridge: Cambridge University Press, 2003. (This is one of many excellent introductions to linguistics and the history of English.)

Leland, Andrew. "DeafBlind Communities May Be Creating a New Language of Touch." *The New Yorker,* May 12, 2022.

ON NATIVE AMERICAN WORDS IN ENGLISH

Bright, William. *Native American Placenames of the United States.* Norman: University of Oklahoma Press, 2004.

Cutler, Charles L. *Tracks That Speak: The Legacy of Native American Words in North American Culture.* Boston: Houghton Mifflin, 2002.

ON CONCEPTUAL METAPHORS

Gibbs, Raymond W., Jr. *The Cambridge Handbook of Metaphor and Thought.* Cambridge: Cambridge University Press, 2008.

Kövecses, Zoltán. *Metaphor: A Practical Introduction.* 2nd ed. Oxford: Oxford University Press, 2010.

ON THE HISTORY OF FOOD

Bennet, Judith M. *Ale, Beer, and Brewsters in England: Women's Work in a Changing World, 1300–1600.* Oxford: Oxford University Press, 1996.

Cosman, Madeleine Pelner. *Fabulous Feasts: Medieval Cookery and Ceremony.* New York: George Braziller, 1976.

Dalby, Andrew. *Dangerous Tastes: The Story of Spices.* Berkeley: University of California Press, 2000.

Davidson, Alan. *The Oxford Companion to Food.* Edited by Tom Jaine. Oxford: Oxford University Press, 2014.

The Good Wife's Guide (Le Ménagier de Paris). Translated and with an introduction by Gina L. Greco and Christine M. Rose. Cornell, NY: Cornell University Press, 2009.

Le Ménagier de Paris. Edited by Georgine E. Brereton and Janet M. Ferrier. Oxford: Clarendon, 1981.

Pendergrast, Mark. *Uncommon Grounds: The History of Coffee and How It Transformed Our World.* New York: Basic Books, 1999.

Pilcher, Jeffrey M. *Planet Taco: A Global History of Mexican Food.* Oxford: Oxford University Press, 2012.

Slingerland, Edward. *Drunk: How We Sipped, Danced, and Stumbled Our Way to Civilization.* Boston: Little, Brown Spark, 2021.

Stafford-Fraser, Quentin. "The Trojan Room Coffee Pot." May 1995. www.cl.cam.ac.uk/coffee/qsf/coffee.html.

Toussaint-Samat, Maguelonne. *A History of Food.* Translated by Anthea Bell. Chichester, UK: Blackwell, 1992. (Now largely superseded by other food histories, but a fascinating, informative read.)

Two Fifteenth-Century Cookery-Books. Edited by Thomas Austin. London: Early English Text Society, 1888. Reprint, Oxford: Oxford University Press, 1964.

ON THE EAST INDIA COMPANY

Dalrymple, William. *The Anarchy: The Relentless Rise of the East India Company.* London: Bloomsbury, 2019.

———. "The Original Corporate Raiders." *Guardian*, March 4, 2015.

Acknowledgments

My heartfelt thanks to the following people:

Super-agent Laura Mazer, of Wendy Sherman Associates, for encouraging me to undertake this project, and Voracious editor Thea Diklich-Newell, for shepherding the manuscript through many drafts. And to Jayne Yaffe Kemp, production editor; Melissa Mathlin, production coordinator; Stacy Schuck, manufacturing coordinator; Mariah Dwyer and Fanta Diallo, publicists; Katherine Akey, marketer; copyeditor Tracy Roe; and proofreaders Jen Noon Hess, Pamela Marshall, and Holly Hartman, for transforming a manuscript into a book.

My brothers and my sisters-in-law, for feeding me every time I showed up: Jim and Toni, Steve and Susie, Greg (who also read drafts and asked great questions) and Suphala (who helped with Khmer words), and Joe, especially for the midnight pizzas.

Friends and colleagues, for their expertise, sound advice, support, patience, endless good humor, and many shared meals (alphabetically by first name): Ann Vasaly, Anne Cavender, Beulah

Colvin, Claudia Ingram, Daniel Kiefer, Elaine Crauder, Jonathan House, Julie Brett Hill, Leslie Brody, Marilyn Donahue, Mary Mohler, Nancy O'Connor, Pat O'Brien, Rich Young, Rilla Jaggia, Tasha Wade, and Tina Dobsevage.

My students over the years, for asking questions, for teaching me to rethink, for their convictions, their courage.

Physicist Katy Grimm and artist Peter Grimm, who sat through many a meal listening to the etymology of everything on the table, who read and critiqued the manuscript, and who are a constant source of inspiration and delight.

And to John for decades of love and good cooking.

Index of Words

About the Author

Judith Tschann is professor emerita at the University of Redlands, where she taught medieval studies for many years and served for five years as chair of the English Department. She received a Mortarboard Professor of the Year Award and a National Endowment for the Humanities Fellowship and has lectured and written for both academic and popular audiences. She lives in Redlands, California, with her husband.